NATASJA HJERRILD ROSENQUIST
& RAGNA MOURITZEN

Flowers, Fields & Forests

Simple embroidery projects inspired by nature

Contents

Welcome

This book is our love letter to nature, to slowness and to the senses, and to working with our hands.

In *Flowers, Fields & Forests* you will find full instructions and templates for 30 embroidery motifs inspired by the flora and fauna of the Danish countryside. This book is for both budding embroiderers looking for specific designs to closely follow and more experienced sewists seeking inspiration for new projects.

While deciding the theme for this book, we kept coming back to the same thing: the natural world. We are both incredibly drawn to the overwhelming beauty of nature and the changing seasons. The crisp, frosty mornings of winter with their peaceful stillness. The fresh beginnings of spring, with delicate light green shoots, full of hope and anticipation. The sun-ripened abundance, scents, tastes and harvests of summer. The last flourish that is autumn, with its warm colours and much-needed spoils.

Working on this book led us to look at nature in a new light. We searched with curiosity for its quirky beauty, and we fell in love with the wild flowers, the weeds and all the life you can find along the shoreline, on the forest floor and in the sky, if you look closely. Our experience is that when you explore the natural world for inspiration, you become a more present and appreciative observer, and you become more receptive to nature's shapes, colours and small details.

This book is also an invitation to be present in the quiet moments. In a fast-paced world, most of us need to slow down from time to time, to do something with intention and to connect with the calm rhythms of nature. There are many ways to find peace and, in our experience, creating something with your hands – such as embroidery – and engaging with nature can provide a feeling of stillness and meaning.

We hope that *Flowers, Fields & Forests* will inspire you to create beautiful, hand-worked embroidery to adorn cherished items. We equally hope that both the process and the results of your embroidery will bring you calm and spread joy throughout your everyday life. And remember, just as things grow wild and free in nature, embroidery doesn't have to be stitch-perfect to be exactly as it should be, to bring peace and joy to you.

Enjoy embroidering!

With love,
Ragna and Natasja

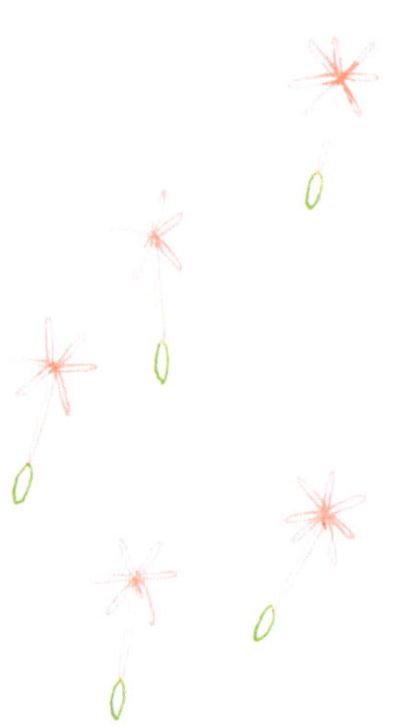

Embroidery for decoration and repair

Embroidery can be used as decoration to embellish clothes and other textiles, but it can also be deployed to cover small holes and stains, giving the garment or fabric a longer life – this is known as 'visible mending'.

We live in a world of overconsumption, especially of clothes and textiles. Giving them a second life by renewing, repairing or embellishing, is a good step on the way to reducing the amount of textiles sent to landfill and limiting the impact of fast fashion.

In our experience, when you work on materials with your own hands, you develop a deeper awareness. You gain a different understanding of what it takes to make a piece of clothing, for example, and a renewed respect for the resources it requires and the people involved. You'll learn which fabrics last well and which do not, and understand how not all materials are equally easy to repair. In this way, many people will gain a renewed understanding of quality, and start to buy less but better, becoming a more conscious consumer.

Whether you're covering holes or improving a piece of fabric with embroidery, your contribution will bring an added value to the textile. When we put time, energy and emotion into repairing, creating and embellishing, we connect with the fabric, we add to its story and we naturally want to take better care of it and keep it for longer.

The embroidery patterns in this book can be used however you wish. As a starting point, they can be stitched onto any fabric as decoration, but most of the designs are very suitable for visible mending to breathe new life into a textile.

Inspiration and process

We are inspired by antiquarian botanical books, and by art, colours and moods. We are inspired by nature – both in the wild and when curated, like in gardens, flowerbeds and bouquets. We are inspired by a rainbow palette of colours, by the contrast of light and dark, by the harmonious shades found in nature. We are inspired by literature, both poetry and prose. We are inspired by what we see in shops, on cycle paths, on the bus and on Instagram. Where do you find inspiration?

We love the entire creative process from inspiration and the initial idea to the finished result. Sometimes the route to a final design is short and straightforward, while at other times we need to re-draft the re-work the shapes, colourways or stitches. Often, we end up in a totally different place from where we expected to be at the start of the process. We both work very visually and need to have the materials and colours in front of us, so much of the design process takes place amidst stacks of sketches, piles of colour swatches and test pieces, and a jumble of different colour threads. Sometimes it's about gut feeling – we can tell when something is going to be good, and we can also clearly feel if it isn't working and we need to try something else. This part of the process is the most fun; it's here that we get to play and be creative. Sometimes inspiration can come from seeing something that we want to recreate 1:1, or life-size, for example a flower or a beautiful shell. Other times, it is small details like colours and shapes that we want to work with in a new way, and that give us inspiration for the next design.

Flora Danica Tab. DCCXXIII.
723
Vild Gulerod
Franske knuder
Bagsting
Mille fleur
Kontursting
Evt. med rodnet ?

STAEDTLER

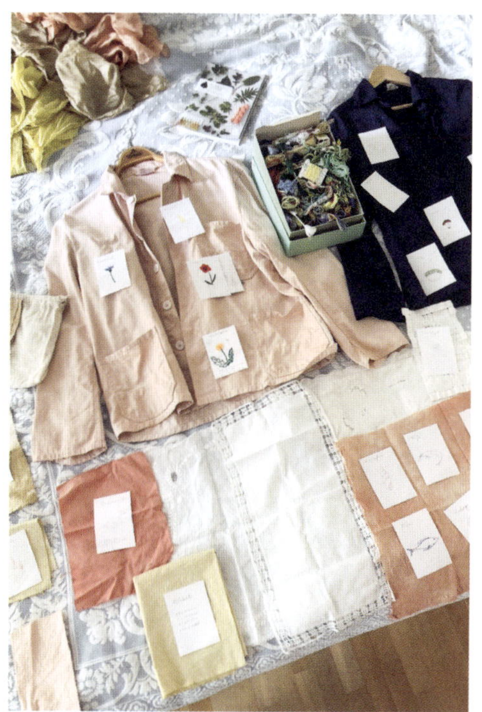

Lademanns naturfører
Farve-flora

Getting started

Introduction

This book is first and foremost a source of inspiration for your own embroidery projects. While these are our designs, we would like you to adapt them to your own needs and make them your own. Whether you're just looking for ideas, or you prefer to follow our patterns step by step, we share some tips on how to get the most out of the book.

6 Needles
JJ18884
Size 18/24
John James
Est. 1840
Chenille
Tapisserie bout pointu
Stickadeln mit Spitze
Finest Quality Needles
6 Needles
JJ19818
Size 18
John James
Est. 1840
Tapestry
Finest Quality Needles
335
734

Embroidery materials

Here is a list of useful materials that will make your embroidery experience a breeze.

- Embroidery hoop (we suggest a 10cm/4-inch or 13cm/5-inch hoop)
- Embroidery thread (floss)
- Large-eyed or chenille embroidery needles
- Tapestry needles, sizes 18–20
- Embroidery scissors
- Heat erasable fabric pen
- Pattern paper or tracing paper
- Solufix embroidery stabilizer
- Transfer paper

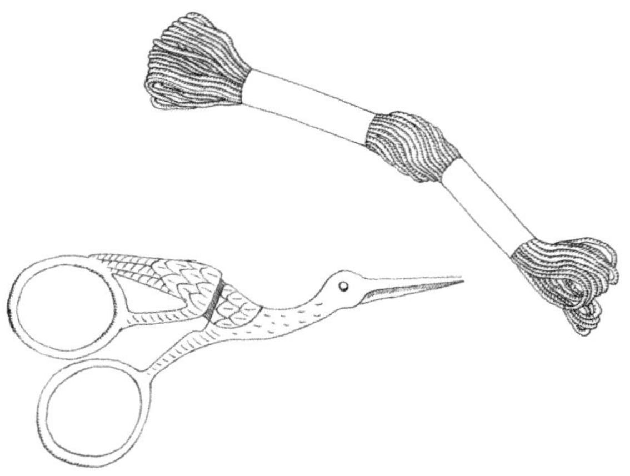

Threads and colour codes

We mainly use DMC Mouliné thread (floss) for our embroidery projects. It is good-quality cotton, which has a beautiful sheen. We love how these threads can be separated into individual strands and then used in ones, twos or threes depending on how detailed you want the embroidery to be. For some projects, DMC's Metallic thread ('Fil métallisé') is also suggested. We've specified which colours are used in the embroidery projects, for those who want to stitch an exact copy, but you can easily find similar colours and get just as good a result. As a general rule, we suggest that you use whatever threads you have in your stash at home to avoid waste.

Note: DMC's Mouliné thread consists of six strands that make up the combined thread. The thread can be separated and the number of strands used can be adjusted as needed, depending on the material you are embroidering.

D·M·C
7
8
9
10
11
828
3761
519
518
3760
964
959
958
3812
3851
955
13
954
913
912
911
910
909
14
15
16
704
703
702
701
700
699
907
906
905
904
472
10
11
12
165
3819
166
581
580
523
配色事典
応用編
大正・昭和の
色彩と
商品デザイン
A Dictionary of
Color Combinations
vol 2
青幻舎
SEIGENSHA

How to transfer your design

There are many ways to transfer a design onto fabric. Here are some methods; pick whichever one works best for you.

DRAW FREEHAND

This will be the easiest method for some, while for others it will prove the most difficult. However, it is a straightforward process and requires nothing more than a fabric pen and a little concentration.

YOU WILL NEED

- Heat erasable fabric pen

Be inspired by our templates, but give the design your personal touch. Draw directly on the material with a fabric pen. Use a heat erasable pen that can be ironed away so that you can easily fix any mistakes along the way.

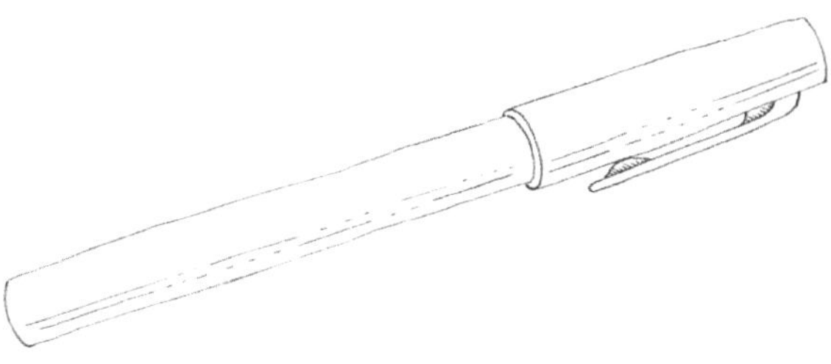

USE AN EMBROIDERY STABILIZER

This transfer method is good if the design needs to be applied to a material that is tricky to draw on, for example wool or knitwear, or a fabric that needs a little extra support, for example if it is very thin or elasticated. This method is also good for those who do not feel confident about drawing directly on to fabric but want to create an outline first.

Solufix embroidery stabilizer (or DMC magic paper) is a self-adhesive, water-soluble transfer paper. You can draw your pattern on the paper, remove the backing, stick it to the fabric and complete your embroidery. You then dissolve the transfer paper in water to remove it.

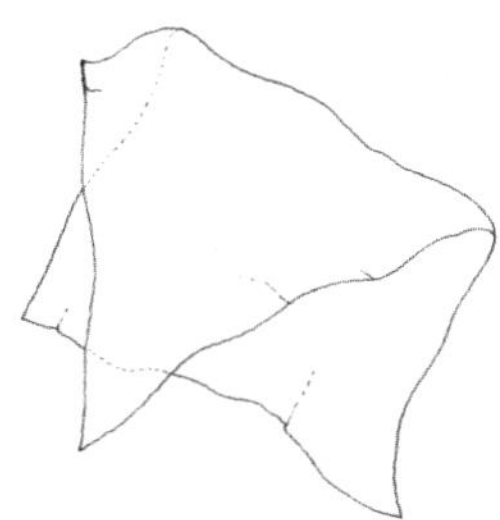

YOU WILL NEED

- Solufix embroidery stabilizer (or DMC Magic Paper)
- Fabric pen

Cut out a piece of Solufix slightly larger than your template. Place it on top of the template and transfer the design by going over the lines with a fabric pen (you can also use a pencil, but avoid a pen that rubs away).

Apply the Solufix with the design to the fabric following the manufacturer's instructions, then embroider over it.

To remove the Solufix, dissolve it in cold water following the instructions on the product packaging.

USE THE DOT METHOD

This transfer method might sound a little complicated, but despite there being a lot of steps in the process, it is actually quite easy and works incredibly well.

YOU WILL NEED

- Pattern paper or tracing paper
- Low-tack tape (optional)
- Pen or pencil
- Fabric pen (preferably with a thin tip)
- Darning needle
- Dressmaking pins

Take the pattern paper (we just use a sheet of tracing paper, it works just as well), and place it on top of the template – you can tape down the corners so it doesn't move around.

Now trace the lines of the template onto the pattern paper with a pen or pencil.

Place the pattern paper onto a soft surface such as a towel or folded dishcloth. Take your darning needle and punch holes all the way around the design every few millimetres (exactly how close together you place them depends on the design).

When the whole design is 'dotted', attach the pattern paper to your fabric with a few dressmaking pins. Now you can transfer the design to the fabric by pressing your fabric pen lightly into all the small holesmade by the needle – this creates a dot pattern that you can easily join.

Finally, remove the pattern paper, then connect the dots with the fabric pen, and voilà, your design has been transferred.

USE TRANSFER PAPER

This method is widely used, so we have included it here. Transfer paper has a layer of colour on one side that is easily transferred to the fabric when pressure is applied.

YOU WILL NEED

- Pattern paper (tracing paper) or plain printer paper
- Transfer paper
- A few dressmaking pins (optional)
- A pointed object (such as a knitting needle or darning needle)

Trace the design on a piece of pattern paper or plain printer paper.

Place the transfer paper on your fabric where you want the design, with the colour side down.

Place your traced outline of the template on top of the transfer paper (you can secure the layers with some dressmaking pins).

Now trace over the lines of the template with a pointed object so that the colour from the transfer paper marks the fabric.

Remove both the pattern paper and the transfer paper, then embroider the design.

Most of the time, the transferred colour will disappear with water when the fabric is washed, but follow the manufacturer's instructions on the product packaging.

PÅ STRANDEN
HIMLEN
I SKOVEN
Søstjerne
Kamille
Svampe
Græs

#1 ARCHIVAL INK
AP
ENGLAND
DERWENT • WATERCOLOUR
May Green 48
ENGLAND
DERWENT

Tips for beautiful embroidery

USE THE PATTERNS IN SEVERAL WAYS

For each embroidery pattern, we've come up with one or more suggestions for how you can use the design in different ways. We might suggest alternative stitches for the design, new colour combinations or ideas for how one or more elements of design can be combined, placed or re-thought. These suggestions are intended as pure inspiration; of course, you can use the motifs however they work best for you.

Remember, you can always adjust the size, shape and configuration of a design to adapt it for your fabric, for where you wish to place it and for your own taste. Every motif can be enlarged, reduced, mirrored, added to or combined with other motifs to make it exactly how you want it to be.

TIPS

- Choose good-quality fabrics, tools and thread – they are more enjoyable to work with and last longer.

- Wash your fabric before use – this will prevent it from shrinking in the wash and stop the embroidery bunching up.

- Divide your embroidery thread into a smaller number of strands – using just one, two or three strands together allows for finer and more detailed work; using more strands creates a heavier line.

- Combine different shades or colours of embroidery thread in the same stitches – this can create a subtle, blended effect that is often more lifelike for motifs inspired by the natural world.

- Take your time, but don't expect your work to be stitch-perfect – celebrate the small imperfections as they are what make hand-stitched embroidery look handmade.

STITCHES

We have put together a library of all the stitches needed for these embroidery designs at the back of the book (see page 168). Instructions and an illustration are given for each stitch, which will help you on your way. If you need further support, we recommend searching for how-to videos on YouTube, where plenty of extra help can be found. There are also some instructional video guides for embroidery stitches on the Lille Klode website: www.lilleklode.dk

Patterns

24
105
105a
106a
105b
106b
106
105. Svalehale, Papilio machaon. 105a larve. 105b puppe. 106. Apollo,
Parnassius apollo. 106a larve. 106b puppe
107. S
storred

Fields, forests and beyond

We have narrowed down some of our favourite aspects of the natural world – found in forests, fields, hedgerows, skies and seas – and used them as inspiration for 30 designs, which we have translated into embroidery patterns. Many of these embroidery motifs are full of realistic details, so that they look almost lifelike. For other motifs, we have taken some artistic licence to create stylized forms worked in innovative colourways. Working any of these 30 designs is the perfect way to practise the library of 10 embroidery stitches given on pages 168–181. Each embroidery design is accompanied by a short description explaining the inspiration behind it, as well as some extra ideas about alternative embroidery stitches and colourways.

In the garden and along verges

Poppy

For us, the poppy is a symbol of mid-summer. These elegant, delicate flowers illuminate the cornfields with their vibrant petals. This poppy is a further development of one that featured in some of our earlier designs. We have given it a little more detail, and we have also provided a poppy seed head design, which complements the poppy or would work on its own.

COLOUR GUIDE

- 310
- 370
- 436
- 779
- 3347
- 3348
- 3354
- 3805

STITCHES

- Satin stitch (see page 175)
- French knots (see page 178)
- Stem stitch (see page 179)
- Backstitch (see page 173)
- Detached chain stitches (see page 176)
- Lazy daisy stitch (see page 177)
- Short and long stitch (see page 180)

How to embroider the poppy

Transfer the design onto your fabric.

FLOWER

Start by filling in the two middle petals with satin stitch (3 strands ●). The satin stitches should be embroidered vertically from the bottom up, following the shape of the petal and letting the outermost stitches slope slightly. Next, fill in the petals on each side with satin stitch (3 strands ●); these satin stitches should come from the middle outwards, so they lie more horizontally, again following the shape of the petal. The middle of the flower is next to be embroidered. First, fill in the small pistil or ovary with satin stitch (2 strands ●) and then make the stamens with an arc of French knots (2 strands ●).

STALK

Embroider the stalk from the bottom up with stem stitch (3 strands ●).

STEM AND LEAVES

Use backstitch for the stems (3 strands ●). Keeping the same thread, embroider leaves with detached chain stitches. Work one stem and its leaves first, then move on to the next one.

STEM AND BUD

Embroider the bud stem with backstitch (3 strands ●), starting from the stalk and working upwards. Fill the bud with short and long stitch; start with the green part (3 strands ●) and then move on to the pink part (3 strands ●).

STEM AND SEED HEAD

Embroider the stem from the bottom up with stem stitch (2 strands ● + 1 strand ●). Keeping the same thread, embroider the outline of the seed head with stem stitch, then fill it in with short and long stitch. Finish by creating the small flower-shaped top of the seed head with lazy daisy stitches (2 strands ● + 1 strand ●).

Ideas and inspiration

- Poppies come in many different hues, so try varying the colour of the petals – from dark purple or blue, through to yellow, cream or white, and the iconic scarlet red of the field poppy.
- The poppy is a defined and very recognizable shape, so try to embroider the contours of the petals (following the lines of the template) in one colour only, using backstitch, stem stitch or chain stitch.

Shepherd's purse

Shepherd's purse is a common wild flower that grows along the sides of roads, in gardens and on sandy plains. We think it is beautiful, with its delicate form and almost heart-shaped leaves.

COLOUR GUIDE

- Blanc
- 734
- 3347
- 3348

STITCHES

- Chain stitch (see page 176)
- Backstitch (see page 173)
- Detached chain stitches (see page 176)
- French knots (see page 178)

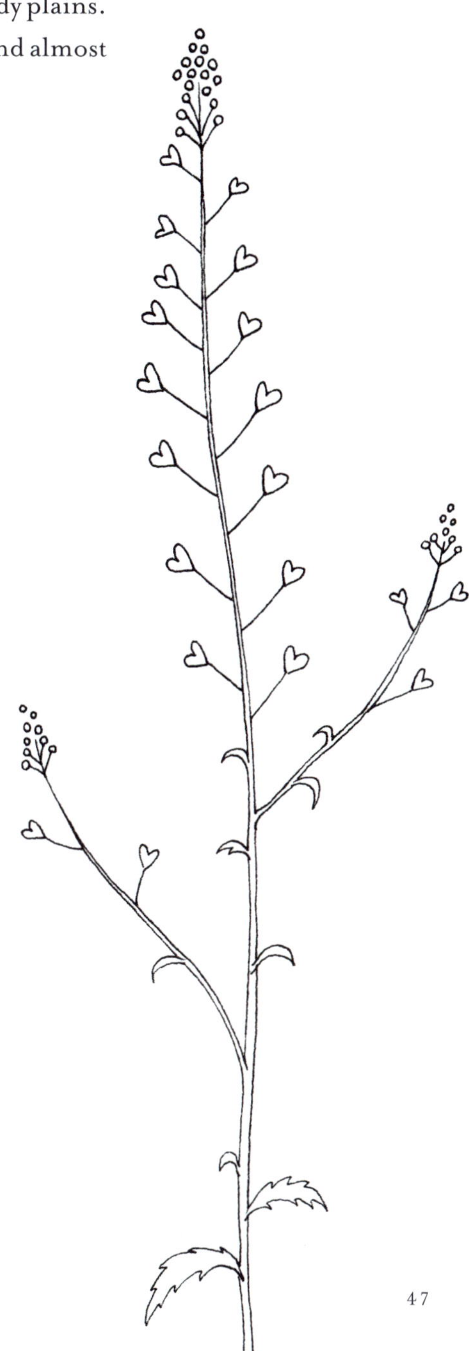

How to embroider the shepherd's purse

Transfer the design onto your fabric.

STALK

Start by embroidering the main stalk and the two shorter side stalks with chain stitch (1 strand ● + 2 strands ●).

STEMS AND LEAVES

Keeping the same thread, make the small stems with backstitch – start stitching at the end of the stem and work towards the stalk. At the end of each small stem, make a heart-shaped leaf by embroidering two detached chain stitches, both of which start at the end of the stem and are angled slightly to each side, to form a heart.

FLOWERS

Now embroider the small flower heads with French knots (1 strand ● + 2 strand ○). Don't pull the French knots too tight or cluster them too densely together, instead allow a little space between each loose knot to create the impression of lightness.

Ideas and inspiration

Work with just the small heart-shaped leaves; sew them in a row, place them in circles or scatter them in a random pattern and link a few with long lines.

Cornflower

Cornflowers are the most striking azure blue and can be found brightening up fields and roadsides. The cornflower is good for biodiversity, as bees and other pollinating insects love it.

COLOUR GUIDE

- 3839
- 796
- 3347
- 3818

STITCHES

- Satin stitch (see page 175)
- Backstitch (see page 173)
- Stem stitch (see page 179)
- Short and long stitch (see page 180)

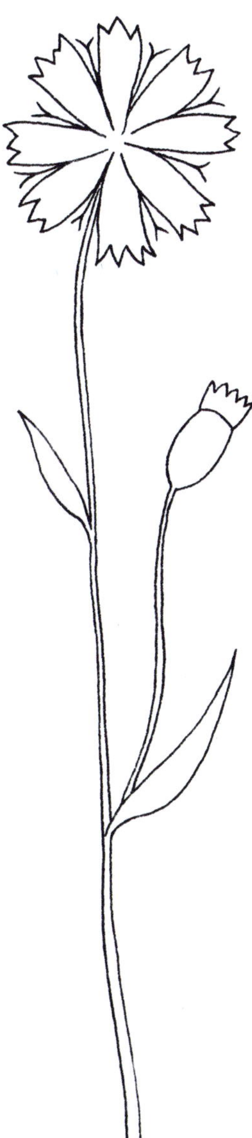

How to embroider the cornflower

Transfer the design onto your fabric.

FLOWER

Fill in the petals one at a time with satin stitch (3 strands ●), varying the length of the stitches to give the petals a slightly jagged look. Next, embroider the stamens also with satin stitch (2 strands ●). At the end of some of the stamens, make a small 'v' with short backstitches.

STALK AND STEM

Embroider both the stalk and stem from the bottom up with stem stitch (2 strands ● + 1 strand ●).

FLOWER BUD

Embroider the edges of the green bud with stem stitch, then fill in with short and long stitch (2 strands ● + 1 strand ●). Let the petals peek out of the green bud in a fan shape with satin stitch (2 strands ●).

LEAVES

Work the edges of the leaves with stem stitch, then fill in with long and short stitch (2 strands ● + 1 strand ●).

Ideas and inspiration

- The petals of the cornflower don't have to be blue; try sewing them in a variety of shades from chocolate brown to light purple and pink.
- Try using just the flower head; either arrange several in a pattern or scatter them randomly over the fabric.

Common sorrel

Once you've seen it, you'll notice common sorrel everywhere. It doesn't look particularly special from a distance, but when you get close, the small, elegant rust-coloured leaves are delightful. It is another beautiful wild flower that is great for biodiversity.

COLOUR GUIDE

- 21
- 919
- 3328
- 3347
- 3348

STITCHES

- Stem stitch (see page 179)
- Backstitch (see page 173)
- French knots (see page 178)
- Short and long stitch (see page 180)

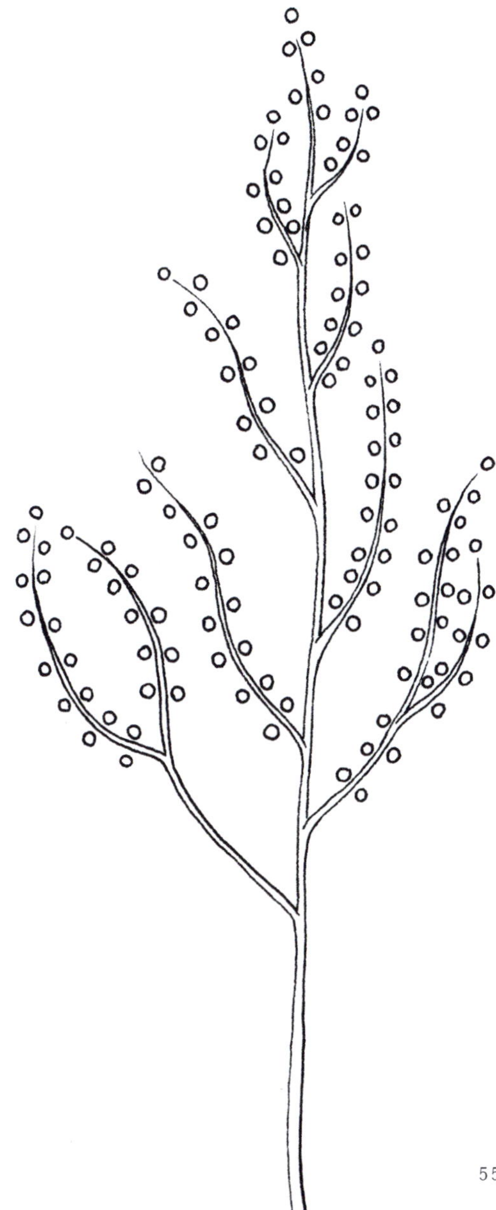

How to embroider the common sorrel

Transfer the design onto your fabric.

STALK

First, embroider the stalk with stem stitch (3 strands ●). Start from the bottom and work up to the top.

FLOWER SHOOTS

Keeping the same thread, embroider the small side stems (flower shoots) with backstitch.

FLOWERS

Finally, make the small clusters of flower buds using French knots (1 thread ● + 1 thread ● + 1 thread ●).

LEAVES AND STEM

Embroider the stem of the large leaf with stem stitch (3 strands ●), then fill in both leaves with short and long stitch (2 strands ● + 1 strand ●). For the large leaf, embroider from the stem outwards.

Ideas and inspiration

- Use individual parts of the plant as standalone elements: embroider small wreaths of flower shoots with buds on them.
- Embroider even more French knots in a multitude of colours to create fuller spires of flowers, which can be contrasted with leaves that are simply outlined in green backstitch or stem stitch.

Dandelion

We love the bold yellow dandelion that springs up and brings a dash of colour here, there and everywhere. It is often a source of frustration for lawn owners, but it is a true gift for biodiversity, and butterflies, bees and insects love it. The dandelion spreads by releasing its seeds, which whirl around with the wind and sow themselves near and far.

COLOUR GUIDE

- B5200
- 17
- 726
- 801
- 3078
- 3347
- 3348

STITCHES

- Satin stitch (see page 175)
- French knots (see page 178)
- Detached chain stitches (see page 176)
- Running stitch (see page 172)
- Stem stitch (see page 179)
- Short and long stitch (see page 180)

How to embroider the dandelion

Transfer the design onto your fabric.

FLOWER HEAD

Fill the outermost ring with satin stitch (2 strands ● + 1 strand ●), varying the stitch lengths to create a more natural-looking shape.

Change the thread (2 strands ● + 1 strand ●) and fill in the middle ring, overlapping some of these stitches with those of the outer ring to merge the colours.

Continuing with the same thread, fill in the final small circle from the centre outwards. Again, let the new stitches blend with those in the middle ring.

SEED HEAD

Fill in the middle circle with French knots (2 strands ○). Next, embroider the five leaves under the seed head with detached chain stitches (3 strands ●). Embroider the small brown seeds that sit around the centre with a series of straight stitches (6 strands ●). Finally, embroider the white parts of the seeds with running stitch (1 strand ○).

STEMS

Embroider both stems with stem stitch, working from the bottom up (4 strands ●).

LEAF

First, embroider the main vein of the leaf with stem stitch (4 strands ●), then continue in stem stitch to complete the outline of the leaf (3 strands ●).

Finally, fill in the leaf with short and long stitch (3 strands ●) – give the stitches some length (5–8mm/¼–⅜in) so they blend together beautifully.

Ideas and inspiration

- Extract just the single small dandelion seed, and play with its size.
- Embroider several of the seeds in a row, in a star shape or as if they are whirling in the wind.

Wild carrot

We think the wild carrot, also known as Queen Anne's lace, is one of the prettiest umbel flowers in Denmark. It is so elegant, with its long stalk and pinkish-white flowers, which are themselves made up of several smaller umbels. It is perfect in a summer bouquet.

COLOUR GUIDE

- 225
- 3347
- Blanc

STITCHES

- Stem stitch (see page 179)
- Backstitch (see page 173)
- French knots (see page 178)
- Running stitch (see page 172)

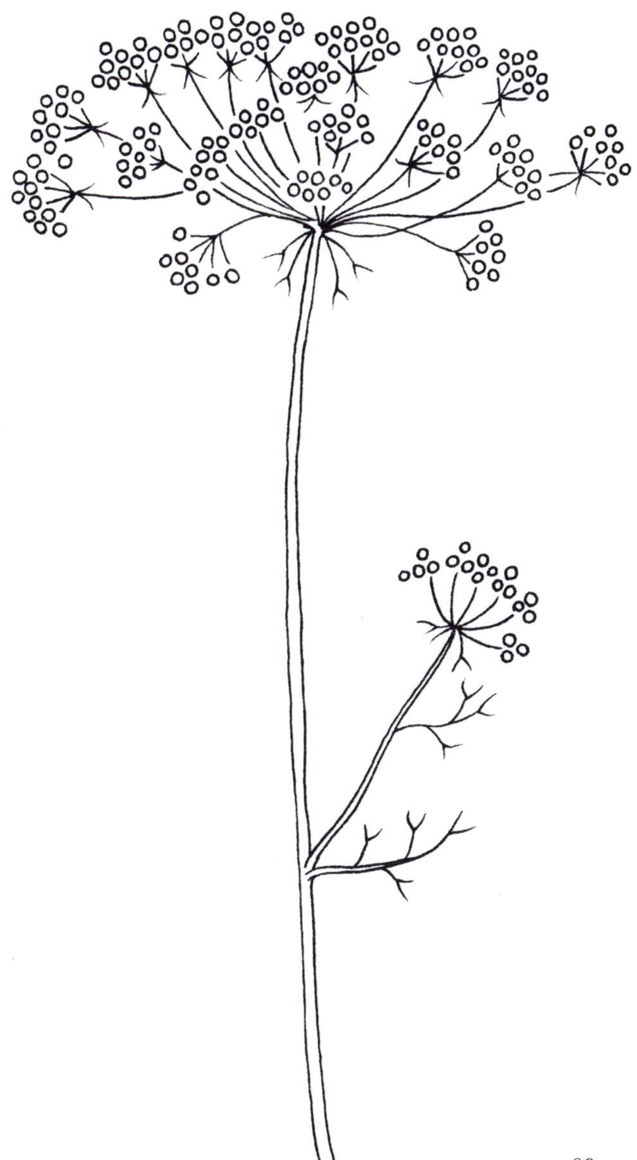

How to embroider the wild carrot

Transfer the design onto your fabric.

STALK

Use stem stitch to embroider the stalk (3 strands ●), working from the bottom up.

STEMS

Embroider the multiple flower stems that which make up the large umbel, then the offshoots from the stalk with backstitch (2 strands ●).

UMBELS

Use running stitch to embroider the small umbels (1 strand ●), then work the flowers themselves with French knots (1 strand ○ + 1 strand ●).

LEAVES

Add the small leaves under the main umbel using running stitch (1 strand ●), then the leaves on the stem with backstitch (2 strands ●).

Ideas and inspiration

- This version of the wild carrot is very detailed, but you can easily simplify the umbel by working fewer flowers.
- Play with the colours of the flowers – for example, mix one or more strands of yellow or pink thread into the French knots.

Coneflower

As well as being a very eye-catching ornamental flower with its warm, deep colours, the coneflower – also known as echinacea – has anti-inflammatory properties and has been used in natural medicine for many years. Even though the flower is not native to Denmark, we couldn't resist including it in this book.

COLOUR GUIDE

- 21
- 335
- 919
- 3328
- 3347
- 3348
- 3607

STITCHES

- French knots (see page 178)
- Short and long stitch (see page 180)
- Stem stitch (see page 179)

How to embroider the coneflower

Transfer the design onto your fabric.

FLOWER

Start by embroidering the petals of the flower. Embroider the edges with stem stitch, then fill them in with short and long stitch (1 strand ● + 2 strands ●). Next, fill the central cone of seeds above the petals with French knots (1 strand ● + 1 strand ● + 1 strand ●).

STALK

Next, embroider the stalk with stem stitch (1 strand ● + 2 strands ●), working from the bottom up.

LEAF

Finally, embroider the leaf. Start by embroidering the outline with stem stitch, then fill it in with short and long stitch (1 strand ● + 2 strands ●).

Ideas and inspiration

- Try placing the petals all the way round the cone for a bird's-eye view.
- Play around with the colours of the petals; you could make them lighter or darker from the middle outwards, giving them more depth.

Grass

Grasses come in many forms as there are a vast number of varieties. We love the very slender, ornamental species with small, open ears that look so magical as they sway in the breeze.

COLOUR GUIDE

- 734

STITCHES

- Backstitch (see page 173)
- Detached chain stitches (see page 176)

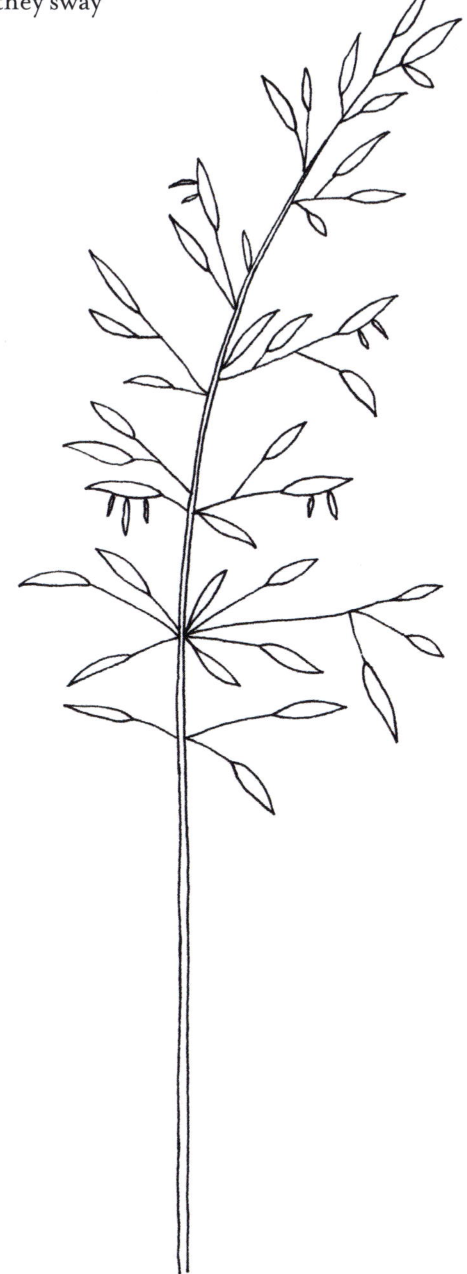

How to embroider the grass

Transfer the design onto your fabric.

We recommend that you embroider the stalk, stems and ears in one go, so that you start your embroidery from the bottom of the stalk and end at the top of the ears.

The entire embroidery uses the same thread (3 strands ●).

STALK AND STEMS

Embroider both the upright stalk and the small stems with backstitch.

EARS

Use detached chain stitches for the ears.

Ideas and inspiration

- Embroider several stalks of grass side by side. Reverse the template to produce a mirror image for some stalks and leave some of the stems shorter, some longer, so that the effect is more natural.
- Experiment with different colours and work the stalks of grass in different shades.
- Create a posy of two or more grass stalks, tied with a thin ribbon bow.

Chamomile

The dainty, daisy-like chamomile flowers are probably best known for their use as a medicinal herb in chamomile tea. It grows wild in fields, along roadside verges and gardens; bees, ladybugs and other beneficial insects love its flowers.

COLOUR GUIDE

- 17
- 3347
- Blanc

STITCHES

- French knots (see page 178)
- Lazy daisy stitch (see page 177)
- Backstitch (see page 173)

How to embroider the chamomile plant

Transfer the design onto your fabric.

FLOWERS

First, embroider the centres of the flowers with French knots (2 strands ●). Next, embroider the petals with lazy daisy stitches (3 strands ○).

STALK

Embroider the stalk with backstitch (3 strands ●), starting from the bottom up; start with the main stalk then branch out towards the flowers.

STEMS AND LEAVES

Use backstitch for the small stems (2 strands ●); start from the stalk and work out. Keeping the same thread, embroider the small leaves, again with backstitch, but with a slightly longer stitch length.

Ideas and inspiration

- Use just the flower heads, worked in a variety of sizes, either scattered randomly or arranged in a pattern. These flower heads can be linked with a series of decorative lines.
- Try using other colours for the flowers – the only limit is your imagination.

Wheat

There is nothing quite as idyllic as a cornfield undulating in the wind on a late summer's day. A single sheaf of wheat is pleasingly decorative, yet requires only two stitches to make.

COLOUR GUIDE

- 370
- 436
- 734
- 3347
- 3348
- 3828

STITCHES

- Stem stitch (see page 179)
- Detached chain stitches (see page 176)

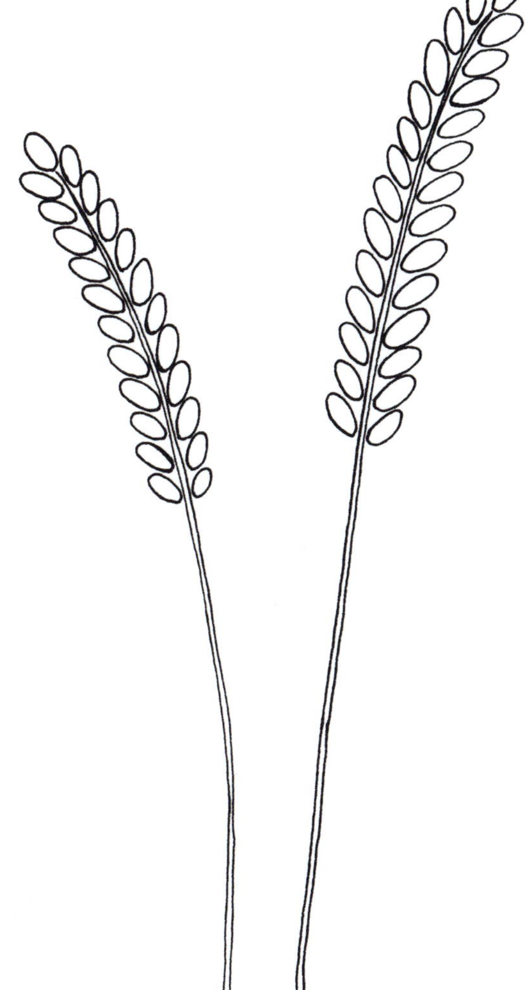

How to embroider the wheat

Transfer the design onto your fabric.

STALK

Start by embroidering the stalk with stem stitch on a contrasting fabric, working from the bottom up.

• RIPE WHEAT: (2 strands ● + 2 strands ● + 1 strand ●)

• UNRIPE WHEAT: (2 strands ● + 2 strands ● + 1 strand ●)

EARS OF GRAIN

Keeping the same thread in the needle, work a series of detached chain stitches for the ears of grain; start two-thirds of the way up the stalk and work the ears of grain in pairs on either side of the stalk, moving from left to right.

Ideas and inspiration

- Try embroidering the grain itself in plain thread – for example, white thread on a dark background or black thread on a light background – so that the beautiful shape of the grain is highlighted and will clearly stand out.
- Easily adjust the size and shape of the wheat sheafs by elongating the stalk and adding more ears of grain to the stems.

Forget-me-not

With its bright, sky-blue flowers, this little spring favourite is easy to spot in flowerbeds and along the side of the road. We can't hide the fact that it's one of our most-loved flowers.

COLOUR GUIDE

- 17
- 153
- 798
- 3347

STITCHES

- Lazy daisy stitch (see page 177)
- French knots (see page 178)
- Detached chain stitches (see page 176)
- Backstitch (see page 173)
- Stem stitch (see page 179)

How to embroider the forget-me-not

Transfer the design onto your fabric.

FLOWERS

Start by embroidering the petals with lazy daisy stitch (2 strands ●). Make the centre of the flower with a single French knot in the middle (2 strands ●). For the small, light flower buds use detached chain stitches (2 strands ●).

STEMS AND BUDS

Embroider the stems with backstitch (2 strands ●). With the same thread, embroider the small buds, also with backstitch. At each of the ends, make three slightly longer stitches to form a bud.

LEAF

Use stem stitch for the leaf (3 strands ●). We have left the large leaf as a simple outline, but you could fill it in with satin stitch, if you prefer.

Ideas and inspiration

Use just the small flower heads, either spread out or placed in a row or in a little wreath. You can connect the individual flower heads with a ring of French knots to make a chain.

Flora Danica Tab.

Along the coast

Seaweed

Seaweed is called 'the green gold of the sea' in Denmark, and there are several good reasons for this. It contains a lot of nutrients, making it a very healthy food source for humans; it is also really good for the marine environment as it purifies the water and reduces the amount of carbon dioxide in the atmosphere, creating ideal living conditions for small sea creatures. Seaweed is really beautiful when you take the time to look closely.

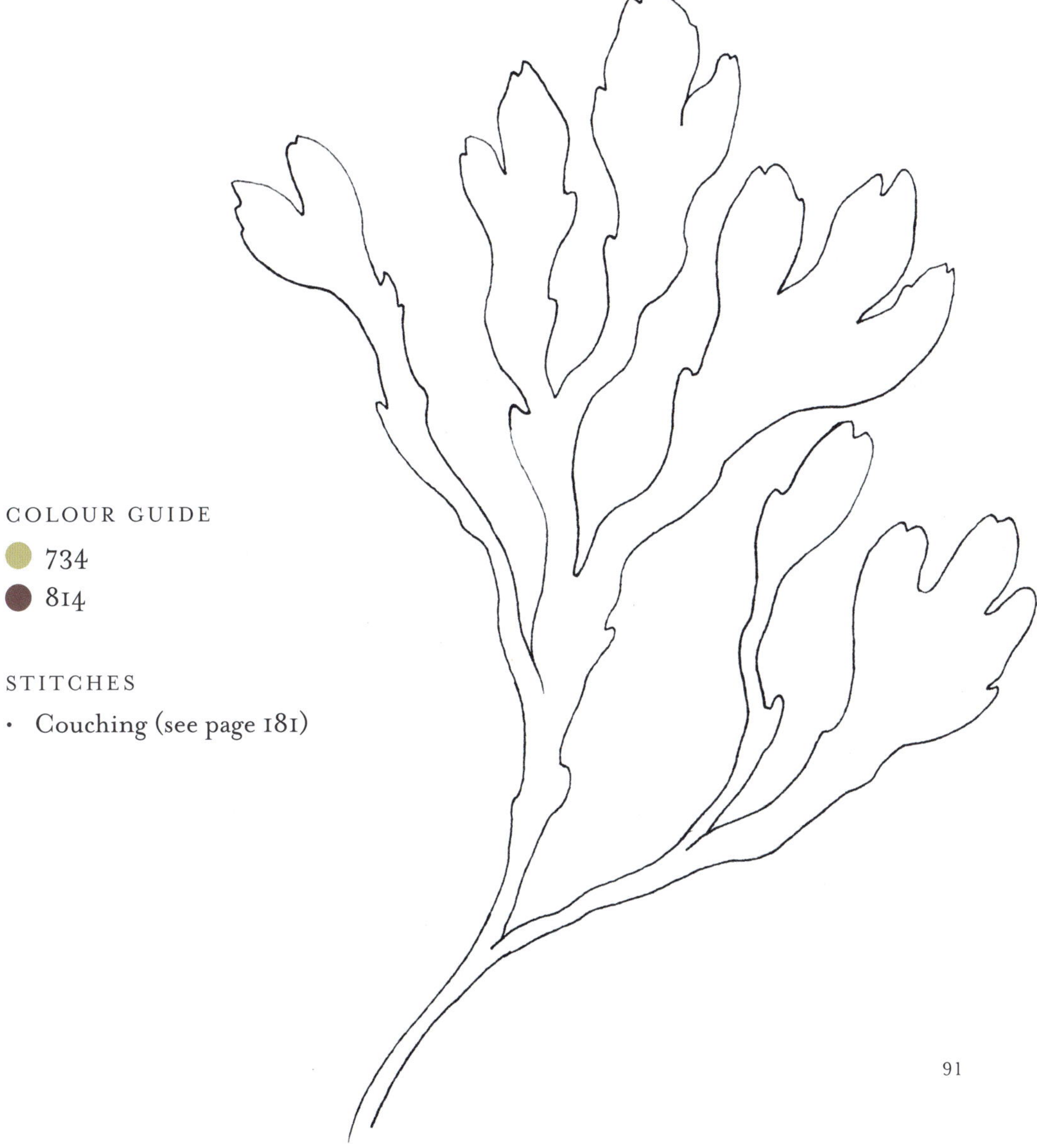

COLOUR GUIDE

- 734
- 814

STITCHES

- Couching (see page 181)

How to embroider the seaweed

Transfer the design onto your fabric.

The entire embroidery is made with couching.
COUCHED THREAD: (4 strands ●)
COUCHING STITCHES: (2 strands ●)

The entire outline of the design is embroidered in one long, continuous run. Start from the bottom and follow the outline all the way around.

Ideas and inspiration

- You can fill the seaweed in for a more distinctive look. Try using French knots or chain stitch, placed in long rows side by side until the outline has been filled.
- Alternatively, you can embroider lots of concentric lines around the outline until the fabric surrounding the seaweed is full of stitches and the seaweed itself remains blank.

Blue mussel

The blue mussel is one of the most common molluscs found not just in Denmark but across the North Atlantic, including Britain and the US. If you go for a stroll along the beach, these mussels are easy to spot as you can't miss their distinctive shells. Blue mussels can shimmer from black, brown and blue to almost mother-of-pearl – they are very beautiful, and no two are exactly the same.

COLOUR GUIDE

- Blanc
- 03
- 798
- 801
- 803
- 3839

STITCHES

- Satin stitch (see page 175)

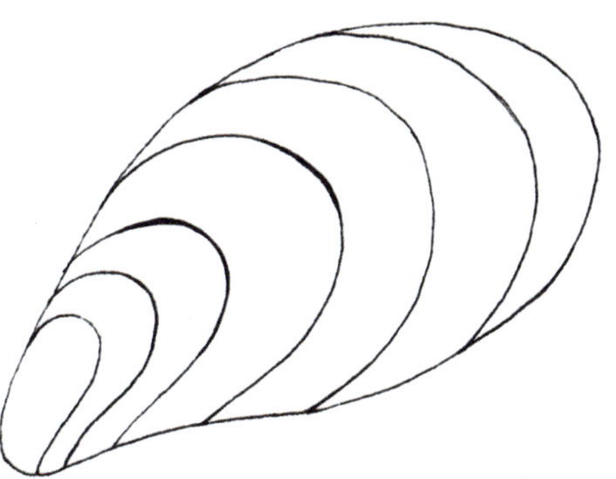

How to embroider the blue mussel

Transfer the design onto your fabric.

The entire embroidery is worked in satin stitch. The blue mussel is divided into sections; start at the bottom and fill in the sections one by one.

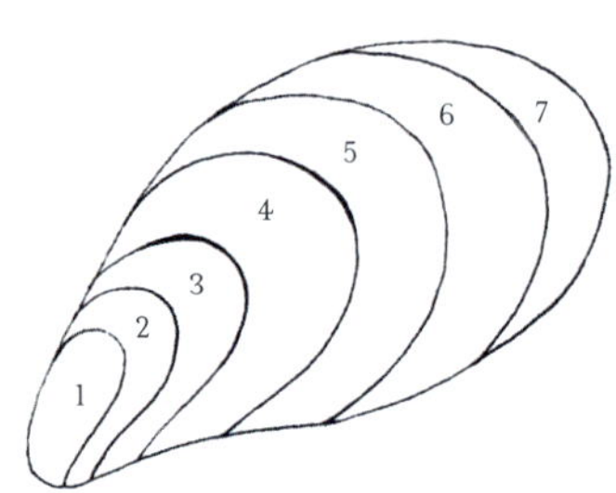

SECTION 1
Satin stitch (3 strands ○).

SECTION 2
Satin stitch (2 strands ● + 1 strand ●).

SECTION 3
Satin stitch (2 strands ● + 1 strand ○).

SECTION 4
Satin stitch (2 strands ● + 1 strand ●).

SECTION 5
Satin stitch (2 strands ● + 1 strand ●).

SECTION 6
Satin stitch (2 strands ● + 1 strand ●).

SECTION 7
Satin stitch (2 strands ● + 1 strand ●).

Ideas and inspiration
You can simply embroider the outline of the mussel; we would recommend backstitch, chain stitch or couching.

DMC:
Blanc
03
803
3839
798
801

Starfish

You may be lucky enough to see a starfish at the water's edge on the beach. They are truly fascinating creatures, but fragile and sensitive to being touched so avoid the temptation to pick them up. With this pattern, you can embroider a starfish that appears almost three-dimensional by using all French knots.

COLOUR GUIDE

21

814

STITCHES

- French knots (see page 178)

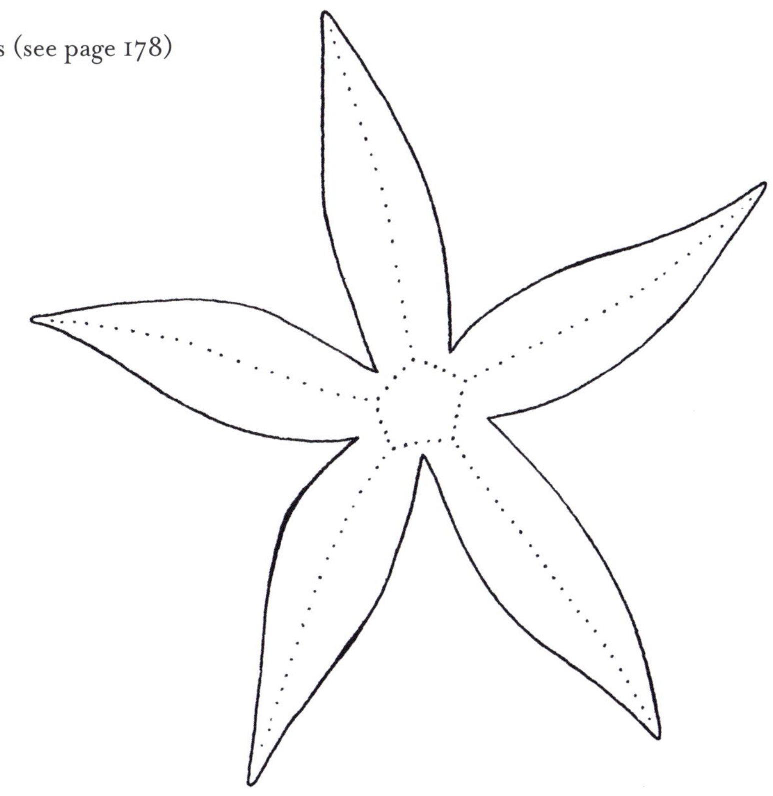

How to embroider the starfish

Transfer the design onto your fabric.

The entire starfish is filled with French knots (2 strands ● + 1 strand ●). You can actually start wherever you like on the design, but it is a good idea to embroider the outside edge first to ensure that it is fairly even.

Ideas and inspiration

- The starfish has a wonderful shape and doesn't necessarily need to be filled in; try embroidering just the outline and the inner details with French knots, backstitch or chain stitch.
- Play with the colours; starfish can have many shades ranging from dark purple to light orange and brown.

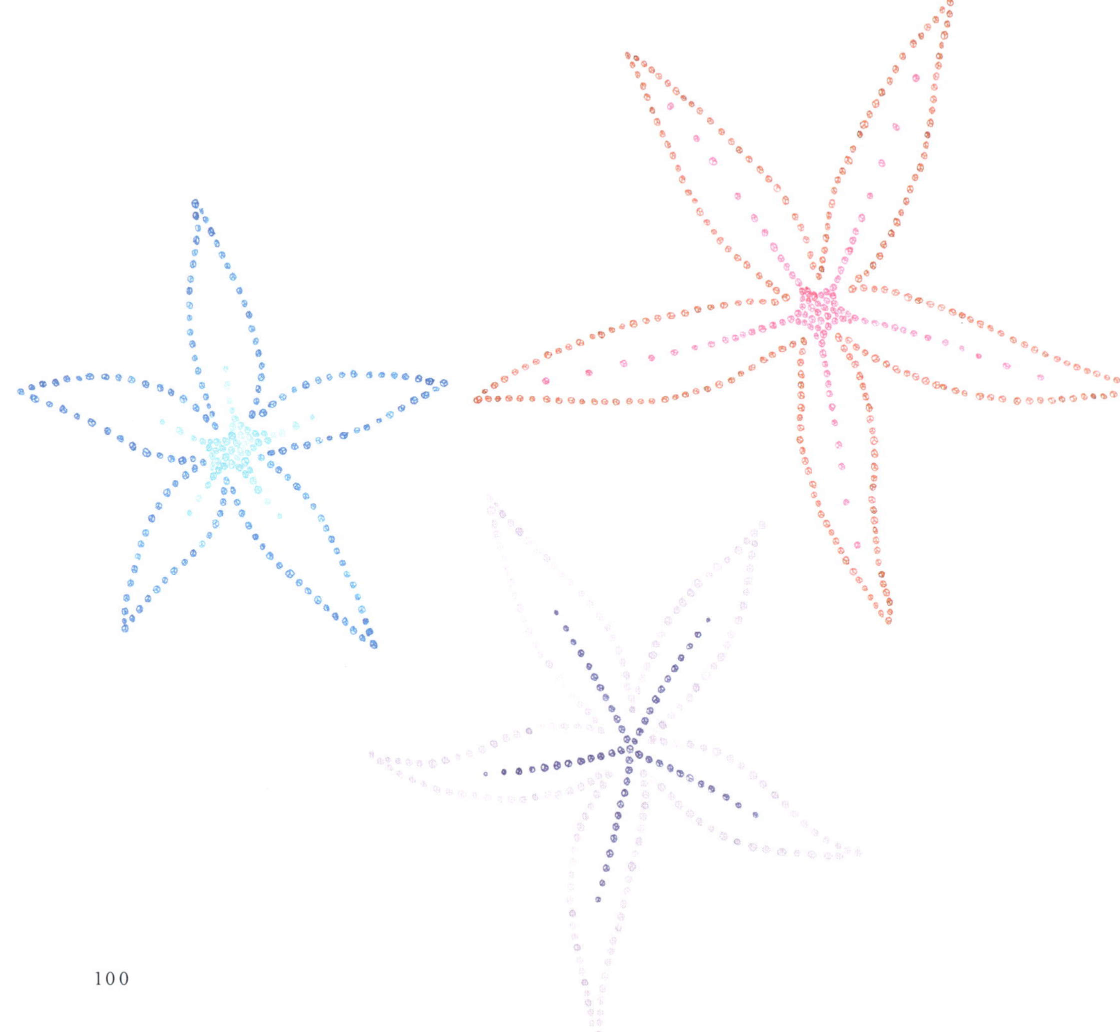

Conch

You don't often find conches along the shores of Denmark, so it can feel extra lucky to spot one of these gorgeous spiralling snail shells. In some cultures, conches are considered sacred, and in other places they symbolize purity and good fortune.

COLOUR GUIDE

 4501

STITCHES

- Backstitch (see page 173)

How to embroider the conch

Transfer the design onto your fabric.

Use backstitch to embroider the entire conch (3 strands ◐). Embroider all the lines in the design; you can start and end wherever you like. Take care to keep to a short stitch length of a few millimetres to keep the curves smooth and avoid your lines becoming too uneven.

Ideas and inspiration

- For this example, we have used a variegated thread dyed in multiple colours that creates subtle colour changes as you stitch, but try embroidering the shell in a single colour such as blue, pink or mother-of-pearl.
- Alternatively, embroider the conch using lots of French knots, but rather than creating a solid outline in chain stitch, use the French knots to accentuate the shadows around the shell and allow the colour of your fabric to define the shape of the conch itself.

8
7

Blue jellyfish

The blue jellyfish is one of several species of jellyfish found in Danish and Northern coastal waters. It is known for its sting, giving it the name the 'blue fire'. Composed of almost 98 per cent water and virtually transparent, they have an otherworldly beauty and air of mystery that is unlike any other sea creature.

COLOUR GUIDE

67

DMC Metallic thread – silver

STITCHES

- Chain stitch (see page 176)

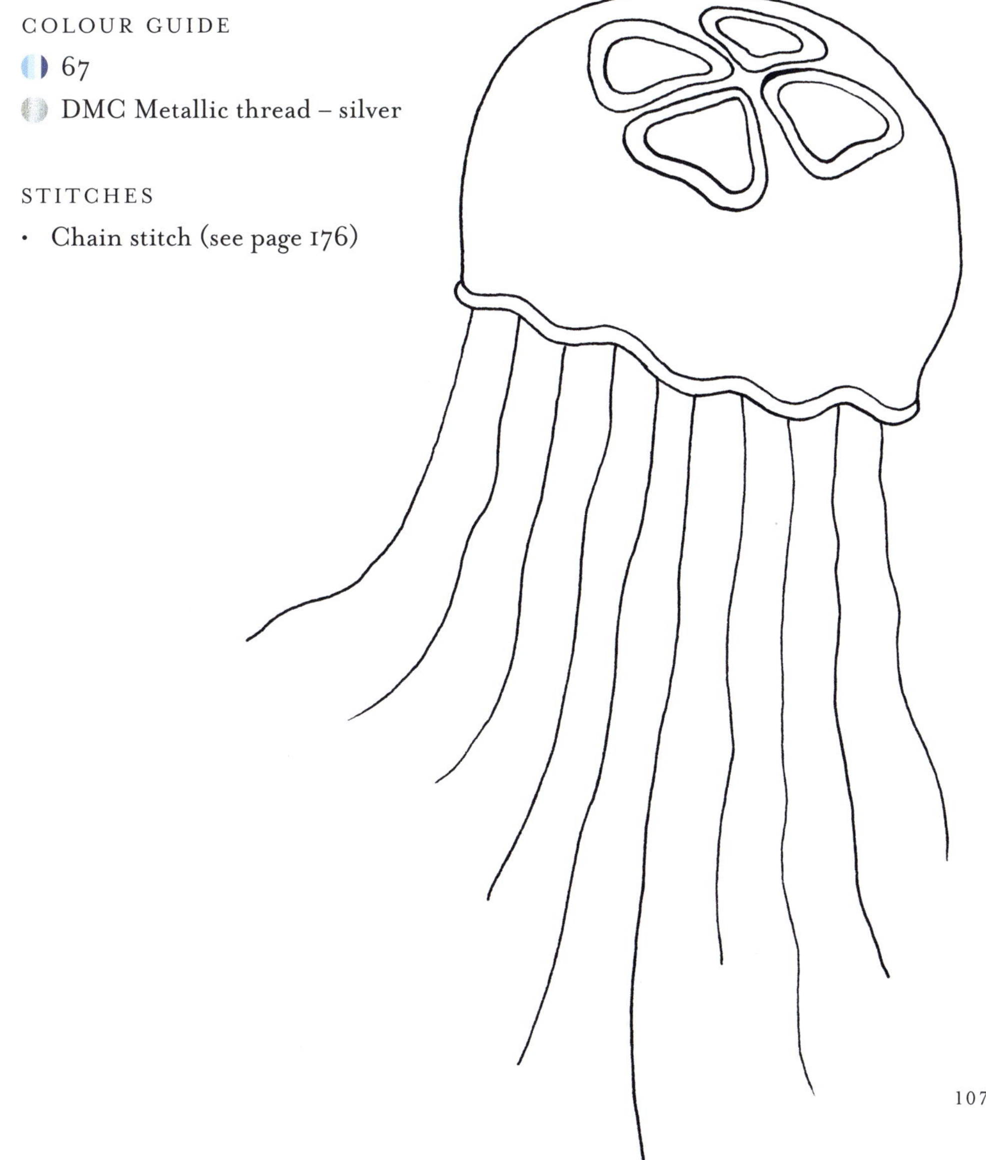

How to embroider the blue jellyfish

Transfer the design onto your fabric.

The whole blue jellyfish is embroidered with chain stitch (3 strands). Start with the body, then embroider each tentacle from the bottom up. In the sample shown, we have lengthened every other tentacle compared to the template and changed the thread (1 thread).

Ideas and inspiration

- Try embroidering the entire blue jellyfish in metallic silver thread.
- Other stitches that would work well are backstitch and couching.
- Combine the blue jellyfish with other embroidered motifs from this chapter to create an underwater scene.

In the forest

Mushroom

The fungi kingdom is fascinating and wondrous. With more than 100,000 species, fungi are found almost everywhere, both above and below the ground. Many of them cannot be seen at all, as they are tiny and grow in hidden places. The ones we know best are those that grow on the forest floor. Their unique shapes and earthy colours lend them a natural beauty – like this magnificent brown mushroom.

COLOUR GUIDE

- Blanc
- 801
- 3864

STITCHES

- Stem stitch (see page 179)
- Short and long stitch (see page 180)
- Running stitch (see page 172)
- Satin stitch (see page 175)

PLEASE NOTE

When foraging wild mushrooms, never consume them unless you are 100 per cent sure of their identification, as many are toxic.

How to embroider the mushroom

Transfer the design onto your fabric.

The template below shows the mushroom divided into sections to better demonstrate the colour changes. Don't make the transitions between sections too defined; let the different colour stitches merge together for a more natural look.

SECTION 1: Fill in the section from the centre out, radiating 360 degrees from one point, like a little star (2 strands ● + 1 strand ●). Make sure that the stitches are different lengths, and extend some of them slightly outside the section outline so that they merge into the stitches of the next section.

SECTION 2: Embroider the top outside edge of the section (the top of the cap) with stem stitch (2 strands ● + 1 strand ○). Fill the rest of the section with short and long stitch. Make sure some of the stitches interweave with those from section 1, and also extend slightly into section 3.

SECTION 3: Embroider the outside edges of the cap with stem stitch, starting where you left off in section 2 (2 strands ○ + 1 strand ●). For the rest of the section use short and long stitch. Again, let some of the stitches merge with the stitches from the other sections.

SECTION 4: Start by embroidering the bottom outside edge of the section (the bottom of the cap) with stem stitch (2 strands ● + 1 strand ●). Then fill in this small section with short and long stitch, letting the stitches merge into the stitches from section 3.

SECTION 5: Embroider the upper part of the stem with short and long stitch (3 strands ○). Use satin stitch for the small 'skirt', using the same thread. Make sure to vary the stitch length slightly so that there is a smooth transition from the stem to the skirt.

SECTION 6: Start by embroidering the outside edge with stem stitch, then fill in the section with short and long stitch (3 strands ○). Finally, embroider the dark details at the bottom of the stalk with long running stitches (2 strands ●).

Ideas and inspiration

- Try embroidering just the outline of the mushroom; you can use backstitch or chain stitch.
- Play with the colours – for example, try creating a mushroom in different shades of green or pink.

Oak leaf and acorn

Oak trees can grow very old and large. You almost get the feeling that they know something the rest of us don't, the way they stand there, so mighty and magnificent, radiating strength, calmness and wisdom.

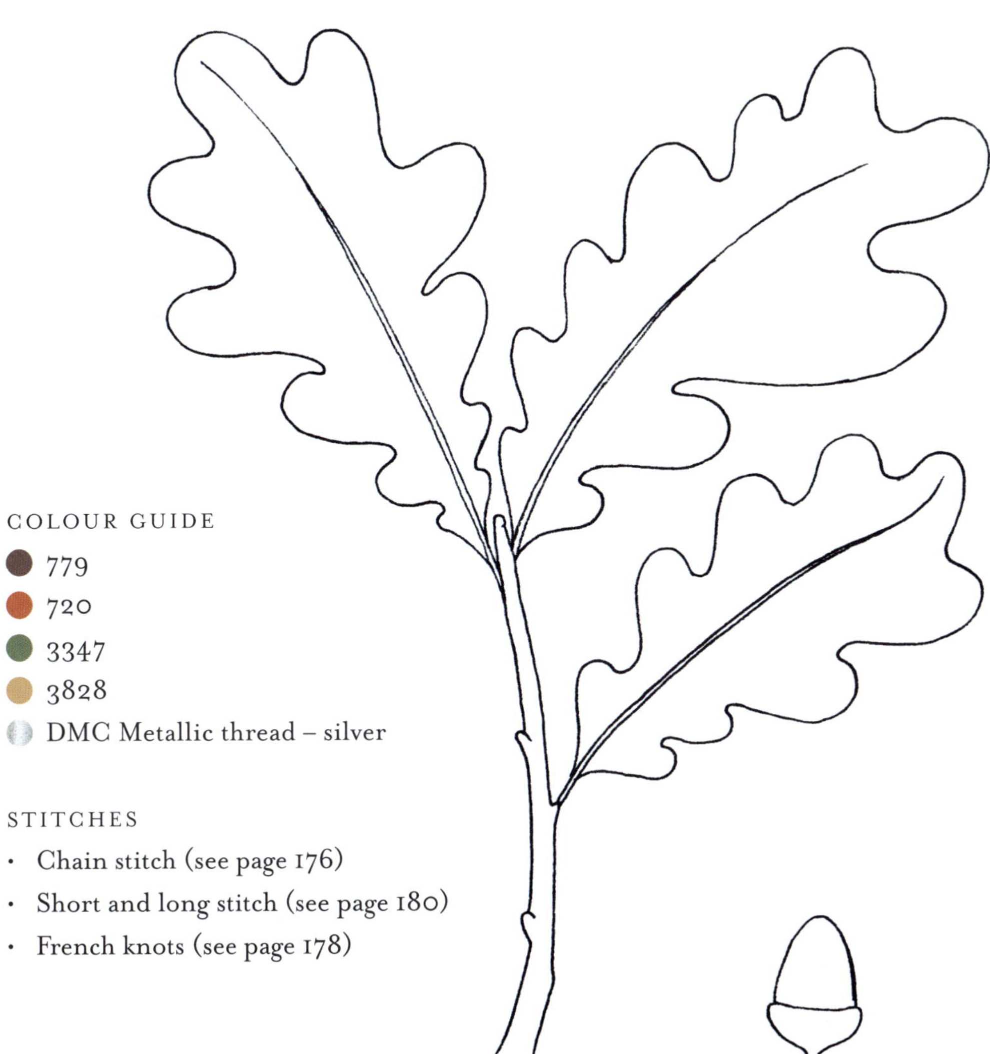

COLOUR GUIDE

- 779
- 720
- 3347
- 3828
- DMC Metallic thread – silver

STITCHES

- Chain stitch (see page 176)
- Short and long stitch (see page 180)
- French knots (see page 178)

How to embroider the oak leaf and acorn

Transfer the design onto your fabric.

TWIG

Use chain stitch to embroider the outline of the twig (3 strands ●). You could choose to fill it in with several rows of chain stitch.

LEAVES

Embroider the leaves with chain stitch, starting with the outline, then the main vein of the leaf.

- LEAF 1: (3 strands ●)
- LEAF 2: (3 strands ●)
- LEAF 3: (1 thread ●)

ACORN

For the nut itself, use short and long stitch (3 strands ●). Embroider the small cap with French knots (3 strands ●). Then with the same thread, embroider the little stem with chain stitch.

Ideas and inspiration

- Embroider the leaves or the acorn separately.
- Fill one or more of the oak leaves with short and long stitch.
- Backstitch and couching could also be used for embroidering the outlines of the leaves.

Raspberry

Is there anything more wonderful than finding a raspberry bush along a hedgerow or at the edge of the forest when you're out for a Sunday walk? We love the contrast between the wild stems, jagged leaves and sharp thorns of the raspberry bush, and the delicious, delicate, soft berries that pop with colour.

COLOUR GUIDE

- 335
- 666
- 3347
- 3348

STITCHES

- Chain stitch (see page 176)
- Detached chain stitches (see page 176)
- Satin stitch (see page 175)
- French knots (see page 178)

How to embroider the raspberry sprig

Transfer the design onto your fabric.

STALK, STEMS AND SEPALS

Start by embroidering the main stalk and then the smaller leaf and berry stems with chain stitch (2 strands ● + 1 strand ●). At the end of each berry stem, make the small leaves (sepals) that sit on top of the berry with a few detached chain stitches in the same thread as the stems.

LEAVES

With the same thread, fill in the leaves one by one with satin stitch. Start the stitch from the centre of the leaf and work outwards so that it is easier to make a neat edge.

BERRIES

Finally, fill the three berries with lots of French knots.

- RIPE BERRIES: (2 strands ● + 1 strand ●)
- UNRIPE BERRIES: (2 strands ● + 1 strand ●)

Ideas and inspiration

- Embroider just the berries – they look good either individually or clustered in a little group. Or, embroider the berries along with the outline of the leaves, rather than filling the leaves in, to really highlight the vibrant berries.
- The raspberry sprig can easily be turned into another type of berry sprig by changing the berry colour to black or dark purple.

Feather

Often exquisitely patterned and highly decorative, it is incredible to think that the feathers we pick up from the forest floor were keeping birds aloft high above the tops of the trees just a short time before.

COLOUR GUIDE

 600

DMC Metallic thread – silver

STITCHES

• Couching (page 181)

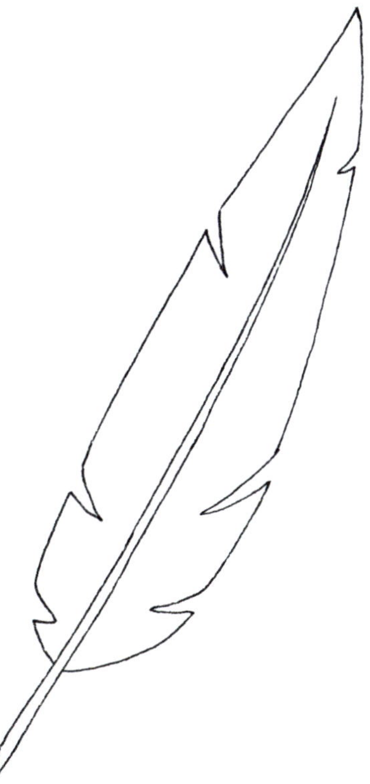

How to embroider the feather

Transfer the design onto your fabric.

The entire feather should be embroidered with couching.
COUCHED THREAD: (6 strands ●)
COUCHING STITCHES: (1 thread ○)

Start by embroidering the central shaft of the feather. Once completed, fasten off the thread on the wrong side. Next, embroider the outside edge of the feather with one long, continuous thread.

Ideas and inspiration

- Try filling in the feather with either satin stitch, or with short and long stitch, if you would like blended colour transitions.
- The outline can also be embroidered with backstitch or chain stitch.

Robin

The little robin is such a charming bird, with its vivid red breast and bright friendly eyes. The robin is known for being very comfortable around people, in some cases almost tame, and many who garden have probably enjoyed the company of a small red-breasted friend.

COLOUR GUIDE

- 03
- 05
- 310
- 720
- 738
- 779
- Blanc

STITCHES

- Stem stitch (see page 179)
- Short and long stitch (see page 180)
- Satin stitch (see page 175)
- Running stitch (see page 172)
- Whipped backstitch (see page 174)

How to embroider the robin

Transfer the design onto your fabric.

The template below shows the robin divided into sections to better demonstrate the colour changes. Don't make the transitions between sections too defined; let the different colour stitches merge together for a more natural look.

All the small stitches can make the design very compact and it may contract a little, especially if you are embroidering on stretchy or soft fabric. It can be difficult to completely avoid this, but take care not to tighten the stitches too much.

BEAK

First, embroider the outline of the beak with stem stitch and then fill it in with short and long stitch (2 strands ●).

BREAST AND HEAD (SECTION 1)

Embroider the outside edge of the breast (below the beak) and head (above the beak) with stem stitch, then fill in the rest of the section with short and long stitch (3 strands ●).

EYE

Work the eye with short satin stitch (2 strands ●). Next, add the little white detail with a single, small running stitch (3 strands ○).

CROWN, BACK AND TAIL FEATHERS (SECTION 2)

Start by embroidering the outside edges with stem stitch, then fill in the areas with short and long stitch (2 strands ● + 1 strand ●).

WING (SECTION 3)

Start by embroidering the entire outline with stem stitch, then fill in the wing with short and long stitch (3 strands ●). Add lighter highlights with a series of straight stitches placed at an angle along the lower edge of the wing (2 strands ●).

FLANK (SECTION 4)

Embroider the border along the wing with stem stitch, then fill in the rest of the section with short and long stitch (3 strands ●).

BELLY (SECTION 5)

Embroider the outside edge of the belly with stem stitch, then fill in the rest with short and long stitch (3 strands ○).

LEGS AND FEET

Use whipped stitch for the legs and feet. First, embroider the lines with backstitch (2 strands ●), and then add whipped stitches (2 strands ●).

Ideas and inspiration

- Use the template and instructions as the basis for embroidering other small birds. By changing the colours and reshaping the wings, body and beak as necessary, you can make all kinds of garden birds.
- The design can be simplified by only embroidering the outlines of the template; we recommend using backstitch, but you can also use chain stitch or couching.

Beetle

The forest floor and fallen tree trunks are full of life if you look closely. For example, you might find the small, iridescent green musk beetle with its distinctive antenna that are as long as its body. These beetles live in willow trees but dare to explore the wider forest in search of food.

COLOUR GUIDE

- 704
- 3345

STITCHES

- Satin stitch (see page 175)
- French knots (see page 178)
- Backstitch (see page 172)
- Detached chain stitches (see page 176)
- Running stitch (see page 172)

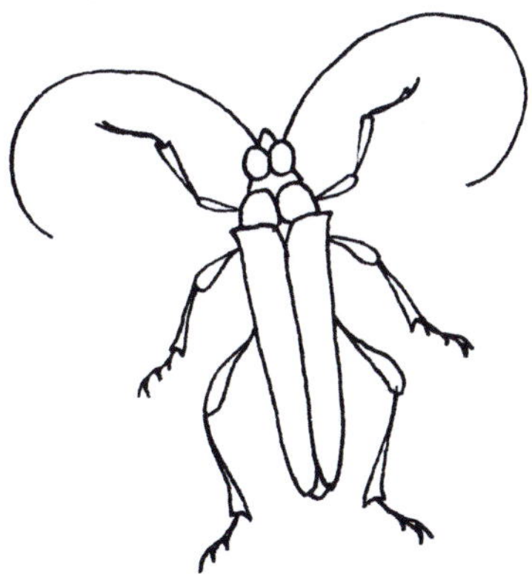

How to embroider the beetle

Transfer the design onto your fabric.

Embroider the entire beetle with the same thread (2 strands ● + 1 strand ●).

BODY

Start by embroidering the body with satin stitch, working the stitches horizontally and from the centre outwards. Fill in one side at a time.

HEAD

Make the eyes with French knots. Embroider each section of the head with short satin stitches.

ANTENNAE

Use backstitch for the antennae; keep a short stitch length so that the curve is smooth.

LEGS

All six legs have three parts. The first part of the leg, attached to the body, is made with a single chain stitch. The second part is made with two (long) running stitches in parallel. The final part is made with a single (long) running stitch.

Ideas and inspiration

- Embroider a colony of beetles that follow a meandering trail of running stitch.
- Try using a different colour for each beetle.

In the air and in the sky

Swallow

We love these graceful little birds that swoop through the air at high speed. Swallows spend most of their lives on the wing, catching insects.

COLOUR GUIDE

● 310

○ Blanc

STITCHES

- Stem stitch (see page 179)
- Short and long stitch (see page 180)

How to embroider the swallow

Transfer the design onto your fabric.

THE BLACK PART

Start by embroidering the outline of the bird with stem stitch (3 strands ●). With the same thread, fill in the whole bird except for the chest with short and long stitch.

THE WHITE PART

Fill the chest with short and long stitch (3 strands ○).

Ideas and inspiration

Embroider the outline of the swallow without filling it in – you could use backstitch, chain stitch or couching. Add dashed lines of running stitch under the wings to indicate the airflow as the bird whooshes through the sky.

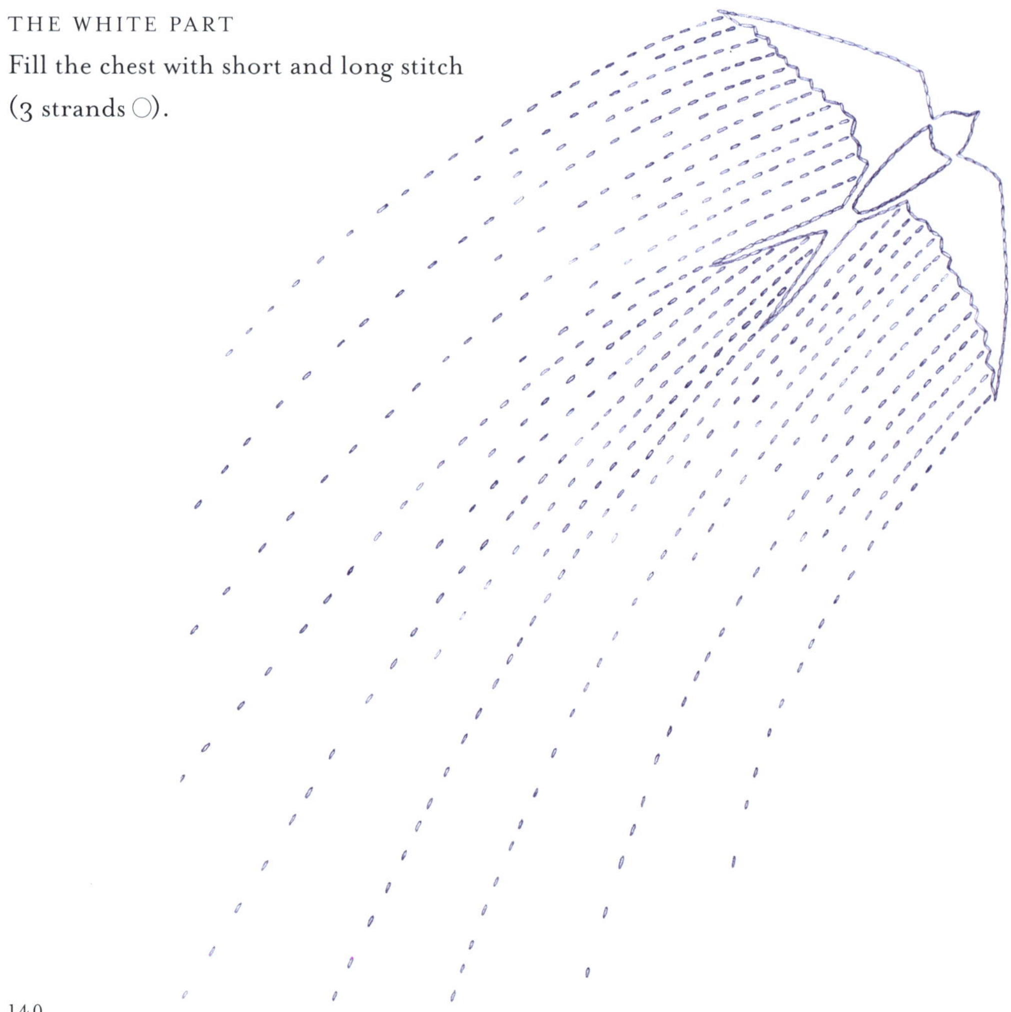

Cloud

We never tire of looking at the ever-changing sky! Lying on the ground and watching the light clouds drifting slowly across the sky has an unbelievably calming effect.

COLOUR GUIDE

121

STITCHES

- Chain stitch (see page 176)

How to embroider the cloud

Transfer the design onto your fabric.

Embroider the cloud with chain stitch (4 strands). Our cloud consists of several lines that end in spirals. Each line should be embroidered separately and should finish inside the spiral.

Ideas and inspiration

The cloud can be embroidered with backstitch or couching.

Sun

The sun can be depicted in many different ways, but at the moment we like this very simple and uplifting interpretation with clearly drawn radiating lines for the rays of the sun.

COLOUR GUIDE

- 307
- 445

STITCHES

- Chain stitch (see page 176)

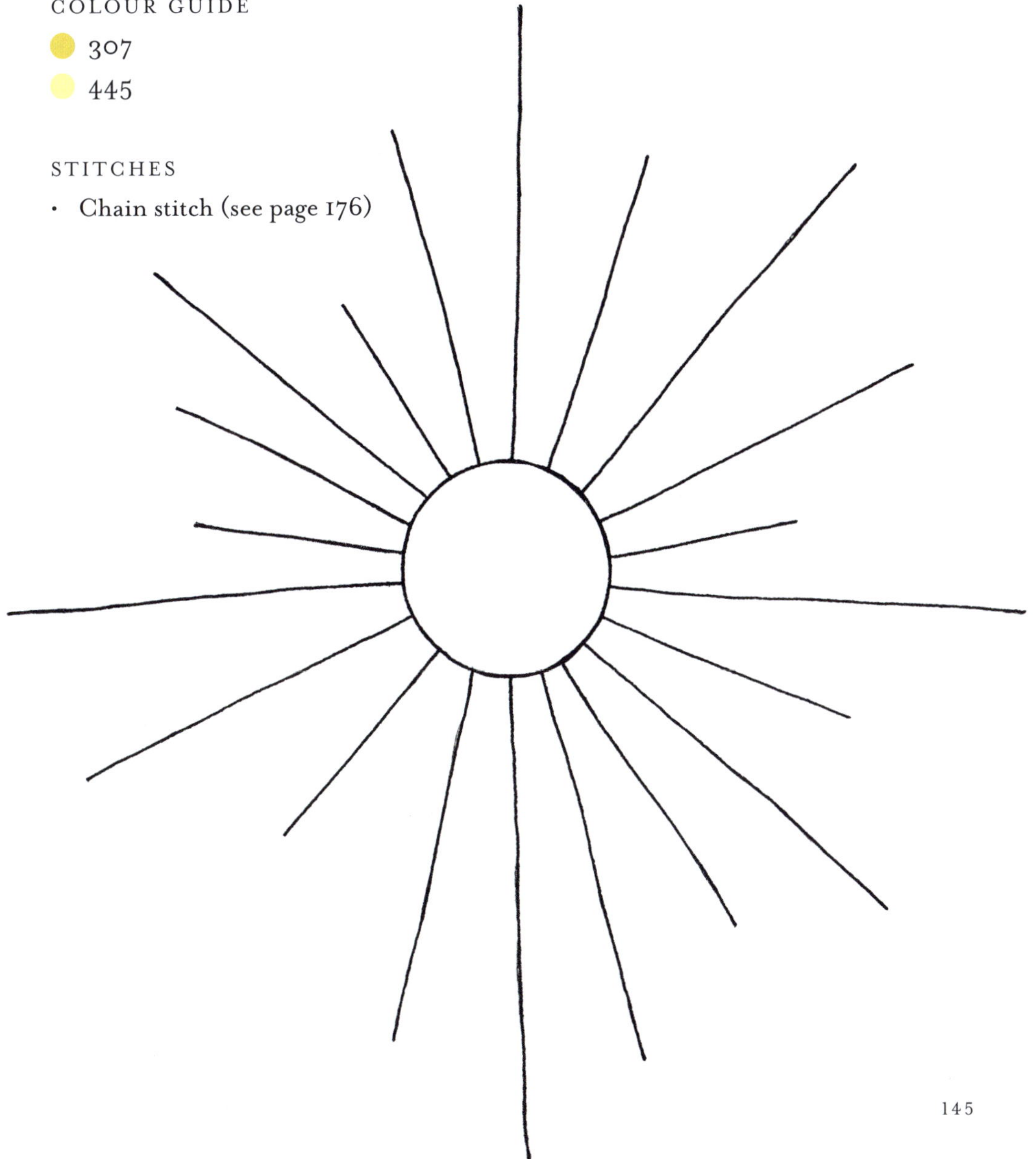

How to embroider the sun

Transfer the design onto your fabric.

Use chain stitch to embroider the entire sun (2 strands ● + 2 strands ●). Start with the round sun itself, and then embroider the rays one by one from the middle outwards.

Ideas and inspiration

- If you want to fill in the sun, you can continue the chain stitch around in a tight spiral, until you reach the centre and the whole sun is filled in.
- The outline of the sun can be embroidered with backstitch or couching.
- The rays of the sun can be sewn in a combination of solid lines of backstitch and dashed lines of running stitch.

Butterfly

In many cultures, butterflies have a symbolic meaning due to their different stages of life, from larva to pupa, and finally to the beautiful butterfly unfolding its wings. Their fluttering movements symbolize freedom, but also uneasiness or nervousness. For us, the butterfly represents the Danish summer, and it is a sign of healthy and abundant natural surroundings. We have chosen to create the pretty Common Blue which is so dainty and simple.

COLOUR GUIDE

- 04
- 310
- 3839
- Blanc

STITCHES

- French knots (see page 178)
- Running stitch (see page 172)
- Couching (see page 181)
- Stem stitch (see page 179)
- Short and long stitch (see page 180)
- Satin stitch (see page 175)

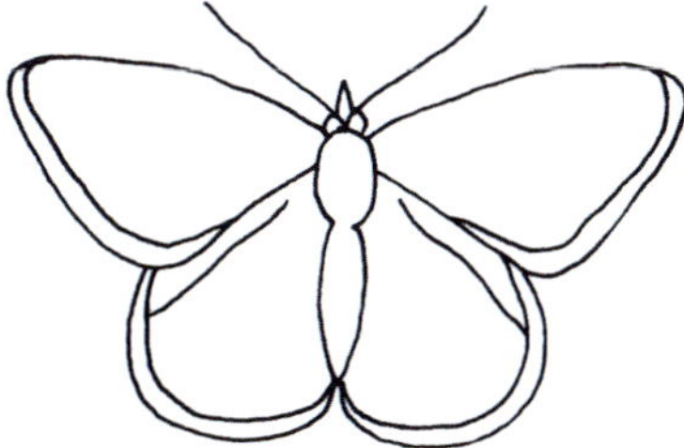

How to embroider the butterfly

Transfer the design onto your fabric.

BODY

Start by filling in the body of the butterfly with French knots (2 strands ● + 1 strand ●).

EYES AND PALPS

Make the eyes with two French knots (3 strands ●), and the palps – which look like a little beak – with a black running stitch (2 strands ●) with a blue running stitch on each side (2 strands ●).

ANTENNAE

Use couching for the antennae (2 strands ● + 1 strand ○). Place a small running stitch using white thread at the end of each antenna.

FOREWINGS

Start by embroidering the inner edge with stem stitch (3 strands ●). With the same thread, fill in the wings with short and long stitch starting from the body and working outwards. Finally, embroider the narrow border along the edge of the wing with short satin stitch (2 strands ○).

HINDWINGS

Start by embroidering the inner edge with stem stitch (3 strands ●). With the same thread, fill in the wings with short and long stitch. Finally, embroider the narrow border along the edge with satin stitch (2 strands ● + 2 strands ○).

Ideas and inspiration

- Use the template and instructions as the basis for embroidering other butterflies. By changing the colours and reshaping the wings a little, you can make all kinds of beautiful species. (See page 190 for more species of butterfly.)
- Try simply embroidering the outline of the butterfly; we recommend couching, backstitch or chain stitch.

NATASJA HJERRILD ROSENQUIST
Nymphalidae Nymphalinae
Limenitis reducta
Leptidea sinapis
Nymphalidae Libytheinae
Libythea celtis

Tocontap
HANOI VIETNAM

Moon

We find the moon is endlessly mysterious and alluring. The moon is an enduring motif heavy with symbolic meaning. In this interpretation, we play with the full moon's outline and lunar phases, but there are lots of possibilities.

COLOUR GUIDE

DMC Metallic thread – silver

STITCHES

- Chain stitch (see page 176)

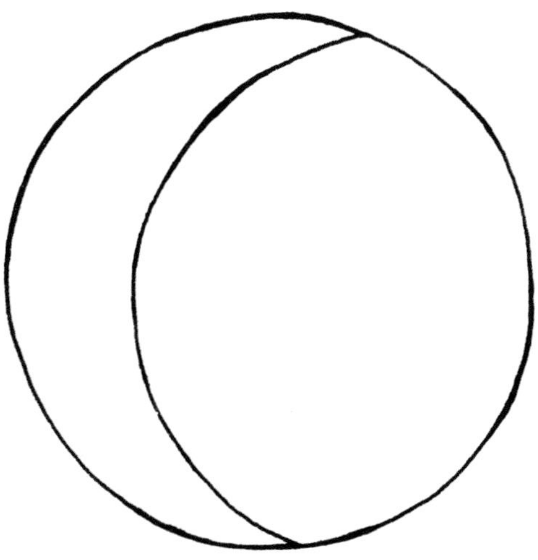

How to embroider the moon

Transfer the design onto your fabric.

Start by embroidering the circular outline of a full moon (6 strands).
Then embroider the crescent outline of a waning moon. Finally, fill in the shape of the waning moon by embroidering close rows of chain stitch back and forth until the crescent shape is filled.

In the embroidered example, we have used a metallic silver thread that hasn't been divided. Metallic thread is a bit challenging to work with as it is stiff and breaks easily, but the result is very beautiful.

Ideas and inspiration

- Play with the different lunar phases and shapes of the moon. You can also skip the outline of the full moon and simply embroider a waning or new moon.
- You can experiment with embroidering the moon in other stitches. For example, it would work well to embroider the outline with stem stitch, backstitch or couching. You can also fill in the moon with short and long stitch, or speckle it with stitches.
- Arrange small crescent moons in a row to create a pretty pattern, or place lots of crescent moon shapes at different angles and overlapping to make a more abstract design.

Dragonfly

With their shimmering, iridescent colours, dragonflies look almost mythical – maybe that's where the name comes from? The dragonfly symbolizes courage and vitality, and its delicate yet distinctive shape is ideal for embroidery.

COLOUR GUIDE

- DMC Metallic thread – gold
- 734

STITCHES

- Chain stitch (see page 176)
- Backstitch (see page 173)
- Satin stitch (see page 175)

How to embroider the dragonfly

Transfer the design onto your fabric.

WINGS

Start by embroidering the wings with chain stitch (1 thread).

BODY

Use backstitch for the body and the tiny legs, using a short stitch length (2 strands).

EYES

With the same thread as the body, embroider the eyes using satin stitch.

Ideas and inspiration

- Try filling the dragonfly's body with satin stitch or short and long stitch.
- Use different colours to embroider the dragonfly, mixing green, blue and silver tones.
- Work extra lines in small backstitch inside the wings and body to add more detail.

9. Vandnymfe,
10a larve. 11.
13. Rygsvømmer.
Gerris najas.
7
7a
8
8a
8b
7a med udbredte vinger. 7b larve.
8a larve. 8b larve med bytte. 8c tom larve-
efter klækning

Shooting star

When you see a shooting star, you have to make a wish! It's impossible not to feel lucky when a shooting star streaks across the sky. Remember to look up at the night sky once in a while, and search for constellations, planets and maybe a shooting star, to remind ourselves that we are just tiny dots in an infinite universe.

COLOUR GUIDE

- 3354
- 3805
- 3806

STITCHES

- Backstitch (see page 173)
- Running stitch (see page 172)

How to embroider the shooting star

Transfer the design onto your fabric.

LARGE STAR

Embroider the large star with short backstitch (3 strands ●).

TAIL

Embroider the tail using small running stitch with spaces in between (3 strands ●).

SMALL TWINKLES

The small twinkles are embroidered by stitching five straight stitches in a little star shape working from the middle outwards (3 strands ●).

Ideas and inspiration

- Make constellations: embroider small twinkles, connecting them with running stitch.
- Use just the large star.
- Use just the small twinkles.
- Play with colours – try embroidering the star, tail or twinkles with gold or silver thread.

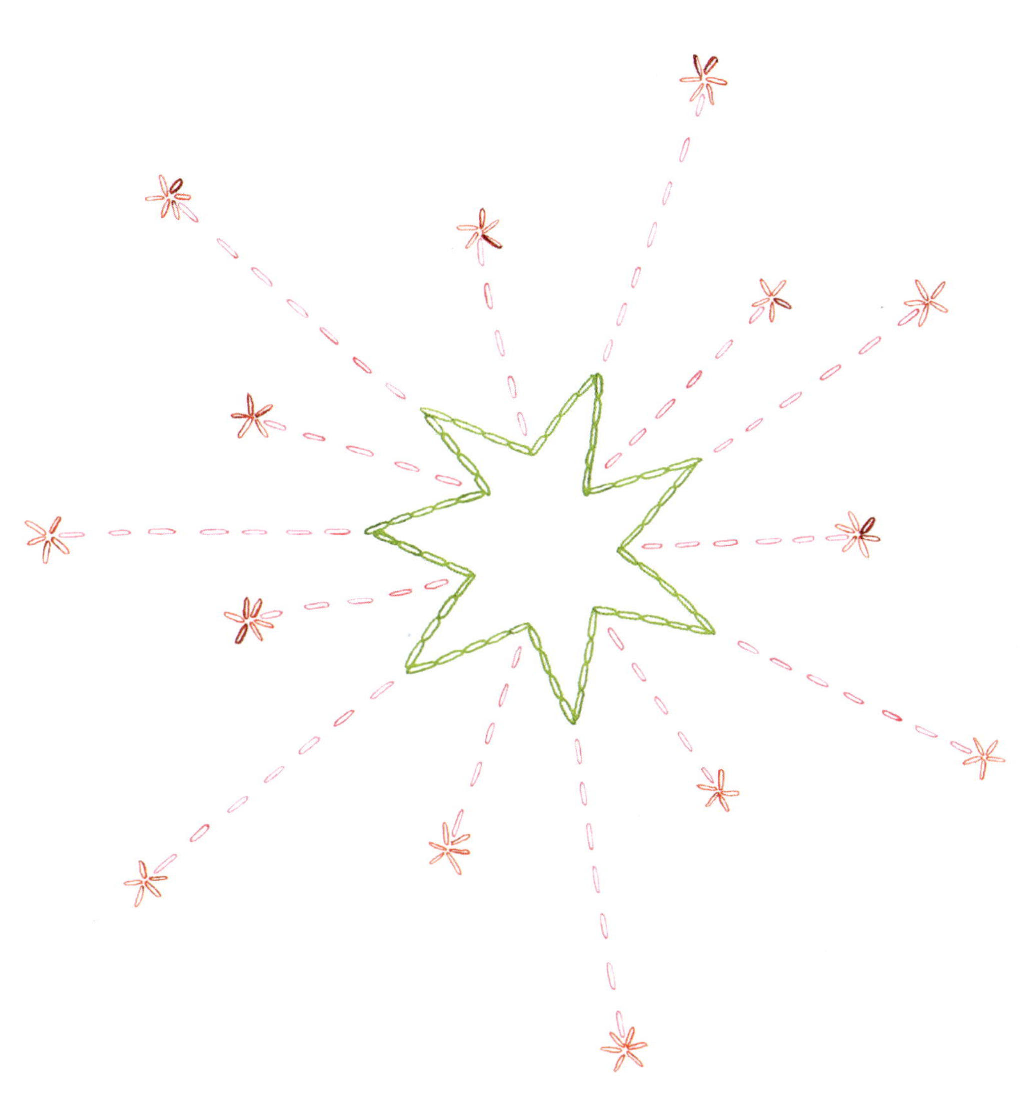

Snowflake

Whether it is fluttering snowflakes in the sky, an icy layer of snow crunching under our feet, or a thick blanket of snow that brings with it a white glow and magical silence, we love all types of snow. Each snowflake is made up of a cluster of ice crystals that stick together to form a unique pattern – in fact, no two snowflakes are identical. Here are our designs for three different styles of embroidered snowflake.

COLOUR GUIDE

- 3841
- Blanc
- DMC Metallic thread – silver

STITCHES

- Backstitch (see page 173)

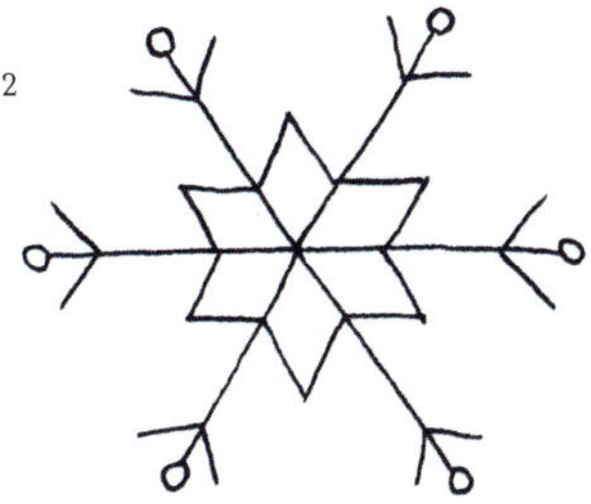

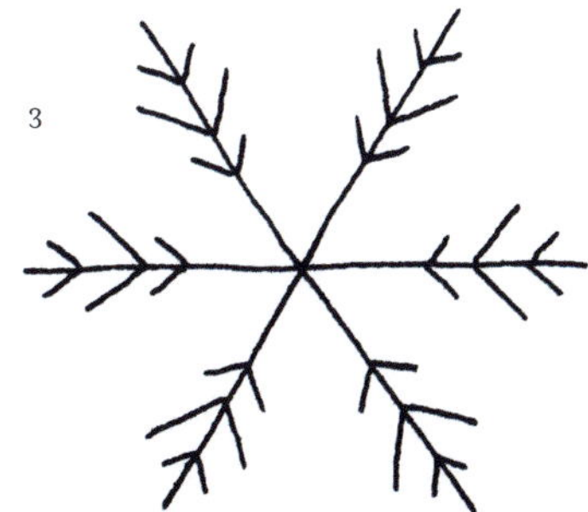

How to embroider the snowflake

Transfer the design onto your fabric.

Embroider the snowflake with backstitch. You can embroider the snowflake however you like, but one approach is to start from the middle and work outwards, embroidering one arm at a time. When you reach the end of one arm and need to return to the starting point, weave the thread into the stitches on the wrong side all the way back to the middle and then start again with the next arm.

SNOWFLAKE 1: (3 strands ○)
SNOWFLAKE 2: (3 strands ●)
SNOWFLAKE 3: (1 thread ◐)

Ideas and inspiration

- Make a small blizzard by embroidering a swirl of snowflakes.
- You can simplify or elaborate the snowflake by removing or adding details on the arms, just remember to keep it symmetrical.

Stitches

Matricaria ch
gtløse kan
den langs vej-
til 40 cm
rvblom-

Stitches

GETTING READY FOR THE FIRST STITCH

For beginners, the simplest way to begin stitching is to thread an embroidery needle and make a simple knot at the end of the thread. Bring the needle from the wrong side of the fabric through to the right side at the point where you want to start stitching your design. Pull the thread all the way through the fabric before making your first stitch; the knot will keep the thread in place. When your embroidery is finished, take the spare thread back through to the wrong side and fasten off the end (see below).

To avoid bulky knots, long threads and messy tangles on the wrong side of your embroidery, you can use the 'waste knot' method. Make a simple knot at the end of the thread and pass the needle from the right side through to the wrong side of the fabric a short distance (about 10cm/4in) from where you want to start your embroidery. Pull the thread all the way through until the knot is resting on the surface of the fabric. Now you are ready to make your first stitch. To finish, fasten off the thread (see below). Return to the knot on the right side, pull it up slightly and snip the thread below the knot so that it falls to the wrong side. Thread your needle with the length of thread left on the wrong side and fasten off the end (see below).

FASTENING OFF THE THREAD

A very effective way of fastening off the end is to sew the thread through the reverse of the stitches on the back of the embroidery. You can weave the thread in between the stitches, or just insert the needle gently into the threads. Be sure to sew the thread back and forth a few times, preferably in different directions. Once secured, snip the thread end close to the embroidery.

RUNNING STITCH

Running stitch is usually the first technique taught during a sewing lesson. It is also known as straight stitch or tacking (basting). Running stitch can be used to make straight, curved or shaped lines, such as an outline of a design. The finished stitch looks like a dashed line, but the gaps can be filled by working a second round of running stitches between the original stitches. The stitch length is determined by how fine and detailed the embroidery design is; the longer the stitch, the less delicate the finished effect. We usually use a stitch length of 2–5mm (⅛–¼in). If you are embroidering a design with more rounded shapes, we recommend that you avoid long stitches as this can result in a jagged effect.

HERE'S WHAT YOU DO

- Bring the needle from the wrong side of the fabric through to the right side at the point where you want to start your first stitch, then pull the thread all the way through.
- Insert the needle down into the fabric one stitch length ahead, then pull the needle until the thread lies flat on the surface to complete the first stitch.
- Bring the needle up again one stitch length ahead, so that there is a gap between the two stitches; aim to make the length of the stitches and the length of the gaps equal and consistent for a neat finish.
- Continue working in this way until you have sewn a dashed line of running stitches all the way around your design. Fasten off the end of the thread on the wrong side.
- If you want to fill in the gaps so that the running stitches form a solid line, add another round of stitches in the spaces left between the first stitches.

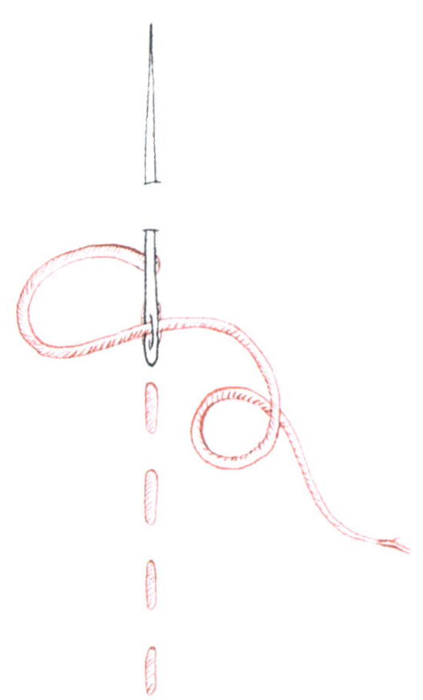

BACKSTITCH

Backstitch, like running stitch, is a very simple straight stitch that is used to create lines and outlines within embroidery designs. Unlike running stitch, backstitch produces a solid line in one go. Your stitch length may vary depending on what effect you are after. We find that a stitch length of 2–5mm (⅛–¼in) works well. To give your backstitch more character, you can add a few whipped stitches (see page 174).

HERE'S WHAT YOU DO

- Bring the needle up from the wrong side of the fabric through to the right side at the point where you want to start your first stitch, then pull the thread all the way through.
- Take the needle back down one stitch length ahead and pull the thread through to complete the first stitch.
- Bring the needle up again one stitch length further ahead. Now insert the needle back down into the end of the previous stitch without pulling it all the way through, using the same hole if you can. Bring the needle up through to the front again but this time two stitch lengths ahead, so that there is an equal distance between the two stitches (see illustration), then pull the thread through. Think of it as repeatedly taking one step back and two steps forward in the same movement.
- Continue working in this way until you have completed your line of backstitches. Fasten off the end of the thread on the wrong side.

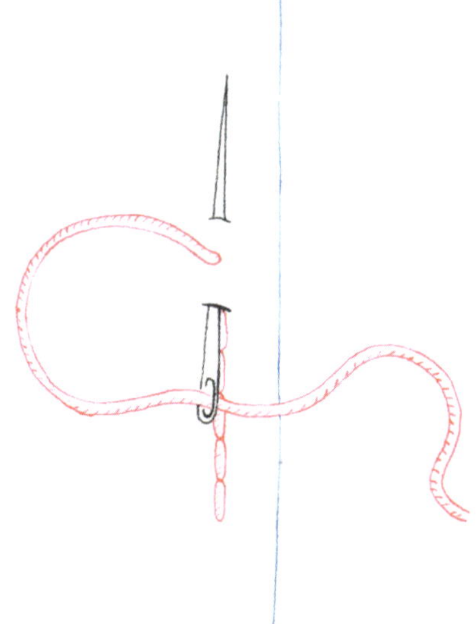

WHIPPED STITCH

Whipped stitch is an embellishment you add to another stitch – either running stitch or backstitch – so it cannot be used alone. It can be especially lovely when used in embroidered lettering and looks stunning if you combine two colours so that the running stitch or backstitch is embroidered in one colour and the whipped stitch in another colour.

HERE'S WHAT YOU DO

- Stitch your outline or design with running stitch or backstitch (see pages 172 and 173) using your first coloured thread.
- Re-thread the needle with the second contrast coloured thread for the whipped stitch and bring the needle up from the back in the same hole or right next to where the running stitch or backstitch begins.
- Pass the needle and thread behind the first stitch and pull the thread through. You can sew from right to left or left to right, from top to bottom or bottom to top, as long as you do the same thing all the way along.
- Now pass the needle behind the next stitch in the row, in the same direction as before, so that the thread 'whips' around the base stitches (see illustration).
- Continue working in this way all the way along your line, finishing by taking the needle down in roughly the same stitch hole as the final base stitch. Fasten off the end of the thread on the wrong side.

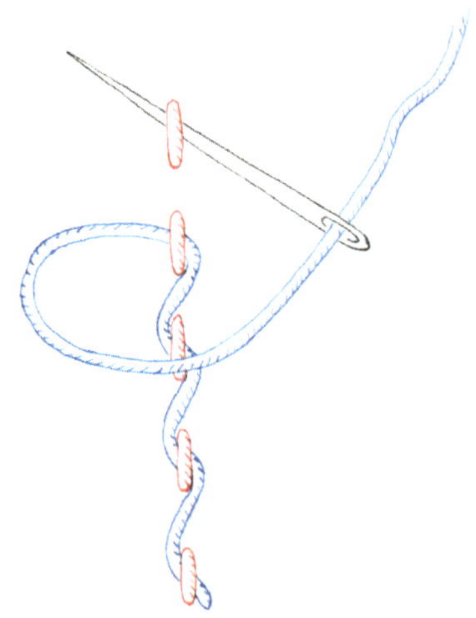

SATIN STITCH

Satin stitch can be used in different ways, for example as filler stitches for smaller areas of solid colour, or for natural details such as leaves and feathers. There are several variations of satin stitch; here we are looking at double-sided satin stitch because it is easy to work and achieve a neat and even effect. Satin stitch can be placed both straight and angled, depending on the design. You can choose to sew from the top down or bottom up, or left to right or right to left, as long as you are consistent with the direction. Satin stitches shouldn't be made too long, especially not on clothing, as longer threads may catch and pull. If you want to cover a larger area with satin stitch, the threads can be fastened to the fabric with small running stitches, which are almost woven over the threads and down into the fabric.

HERE'S WHAT YOU DO

- Bring the needle up from the wrong side of the fabric through to the right side at the point where you want to start your first stitch on the edge of your shape, then pull the thread all the way through. Take the needle back down directly opposite on the other side of the shape, so that the thread runs from one side to the other, then pull so the thread lies flat on the fabric surface.
- Return the needle to the first side and repeat the process, placing the next stitch very close to the first one.
- Continue working in this way, following the edge of the shape, working close, parallel stitches across the design. Take care to always work in the same direction, so that both the front and back sides are neatly covered.
- Continue working satin stitch, until the whole design or chosen surface area is covered. Fasten off the end of the thread on the wrong side.

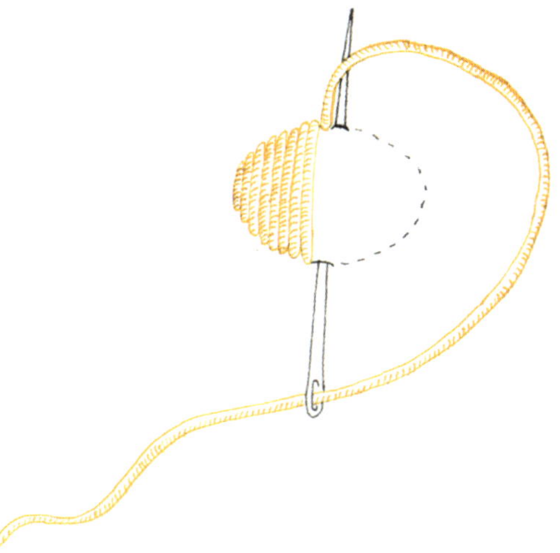

CHAIN STITCH

The classic chain stitch is an elegant and very versatile embroidery stitch. The chain can be made nice and tight with just one or two strands of thread, but you can also make a thicker, bolder chain with more strands. The shorter the stitch length, the finer and more detailed the end result. Chain stitch can be sewn either towards or away from you. In the example shown below, the stitches are sewn away, or upwards.

HERE'S WHAT YOU DO

- Bring the needle up from the wrong side of the fabric through to the right side at the point where you want to start your first stitch, then pull the thread all the way through.
- Insert the needle back down directly next to the first hole, do not pull the length of thread through, but bring the tip of the needle up one stitch length ahead. The distance between where the needle is inserted and brought back up determines your stitch length and how loose or tight the links will be in the chain, and therefore the overall look.
- With the thread running from left to right, take the loop of thread under the tip of the needle and then pull the needle and thread through to form the loop. Feel free to pull the thread a little taut to make sure the loop is secure.
- Now insert the needle down into the same hole where you brought the thread up – inside the loop you just made – and again bring the needle up one stitch length further forward.
- Take the thread under the tip of the needle, from left to right, and pull the needle through the loop again.
- Continue working in this way, making more loops until the chain is the required length.
- To complete the chain, place a small stitch across the top of the last loop to hold it in place. Fasten off the end of the thread on the wrong side.

DETACHED CHAIN STITCHES

When referring to 'detached chain stitches', we mean that each individual loop is finished with a small stitch at the top, just as you do with lazy daisy stitches (see opposite).

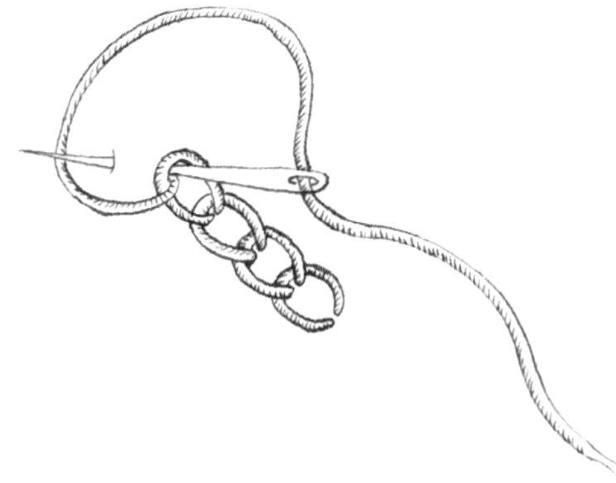

LAZY DAISY STITCH

Lazy daisy stitch is one of our favourite embroidery stitches. It is simple but very charming, and quickly looks like finished embroidery. The lazy daisy stitch consists of detached chain stitches and is used to make petals or small leaves, or a flower head when worked in a circle. Lazy daisy flowers can be varied with many different colours, sizes and compositions.

HERE'S WHAT YOU DO

- Bring the needle up from the wrong side of the fabric through to the right side at the point where you want to start your first stitch, then pull the thread all the way through.
- Insert the needle back down directly next to the first hole, and bring the tip of the needle up one stitch length ahead. The distance between where the needle is inserted and brought back up determines how long the petals will be.
- With the thread running from left to right, take the loop of thread under the tip of the needle and then pull the needle through to form a loop. Don't pull the thread too taut, but let the petal have some shape.
- To secure the loop, make a small stitch across the top of the loop, taking the needle back down to the wrong side.
- Continue working in this way to make the next petal, working in a circle, until the loops form a flower. Fasten off the end of the thread on the wrong side.

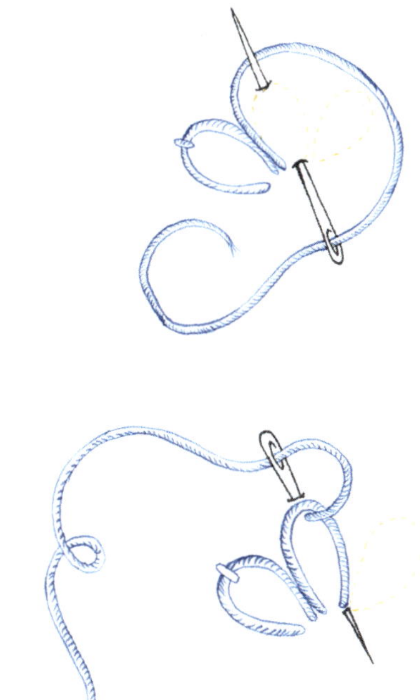

FRENCH KNOTS

French knots are small, fine knots that sit raised on the fabric surface and add texture to embroidery. They can be used for different things, but are often placed in the middle of a flower, as buds on an umbel flower or as other details such as dots or eyes. You can make the knots smaller or larger by varying the number of strands in the length of thread; the more strands, the larger the knots, and the fewer strands, the smaller the knots. You can also make the knots larger with the number of times you wrap the thread around the needle before pulling the thread through.

HERE'S WHAT YOU DO

- Bring the needle up from the wrong side of the fabric through to the right side at the point where you want to make the knot, then pull the thread all the way through.
- Hold the thread taut and at a slight angle from the fabric with the thumb and forefinger of your non-sewing hand.
- With the needle pointing away from you, wrap the thread two or three times around the shaft of the needle.
- Keeping the thread taut with your non-sewing hand, use the forefinger of your sewing hand to move the wraps further down the needle so that they bunch up.
- Now insert the tip of the needle back down through the fabric, right next to the hole where the thread comes up.
- Carefully pull the needle and thread all the way through to the wrong side until there is a small knot sitting on the fabric surface. Continue working in this way to add more knots where required. Fasten off the end of the thread on the wrong side.

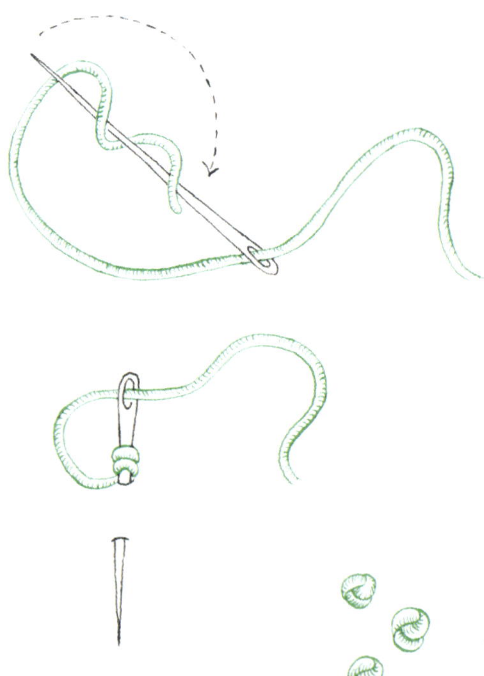

STEM STITCH

Stem stitch is good for following contours. It can be used for the outline of a design, and – as the name suggests – for stems and stalks. Stem stitch is sewn upwards and away from you, but the direction of the needle points down. Stem stitch can be sewn both right facing and left facing; the important thing is that you are consistent and always have the thread on the same side of the needle. In the instructions below, we are sewing left facing, so the thread is always on the left side of the needle.

HERE'S WHAT YOU DO

- Bring the needle up from the wrong side of the fabric through to the right side at the point where you want to make the first stitch, then pull the thread all the way through.
- Make a small straight stitch, then pull the thread all the way through to the back.
- Now bring the needle back up to the front, about halfway along the first stitch, on the right-hand side. Make sure that the thread is to the left of the needle, then pull through.
- Now make a backstitch that ends at the top of the previous stitch.
- Continue working in this way to make more stem stitches, keeping the thread to the left of the needle, going forward one stitch length and then ending the backstitch at the top of the previous stitch.
- Fasten off the end of the thread on the wrong side.

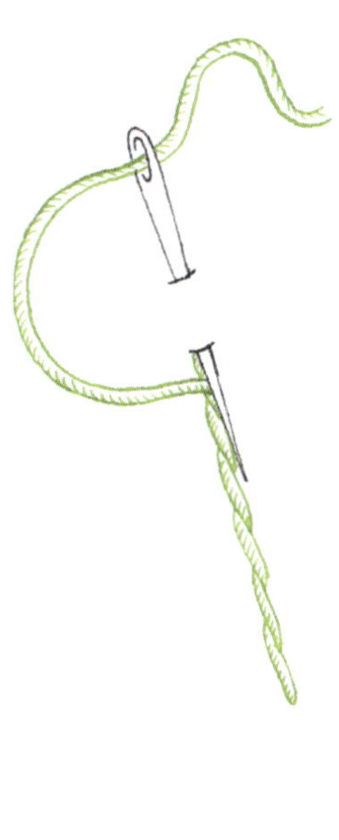

SHORT AND LONG STITCH

Short and long stitch, like satin stitch, falls into the category of filling stitches. It consists of several stitches of differing lengths, which are worked very close together and in the same direction. The stitches interlock to form a solid block of colour, but one with more texture than uniform satin stitch. It is an especially useful stitch for embroidering natural elements, like leaves, flowers or feathers, as it is possible to blend different shades or colours into each other in a subtle way. There are no rules for which direction to place your stitches, but it is a good idea to start somewhere at the edge of your design and then work your way either up or down and out to the sides.

HERE'S WHAT YOU DO

- Bring the needle up from the wrong side of the fabric through to the right side at the point where you want to make the first stitch, then pull the thread all the way through.
- Sew the first straight stitch – the stitch can be sewn as either running stitch or backstitch (see pages 172 and 173).
- Working in rows, place the next stitch alongside the first stitch, keeping them close together and making the second stitch either shorter or longer than the first. The stitch lengths can vary from 3mm–1cm (1⁄8–3⁄8in) depending on the effect you want.
- Continue working in this way across the row, alternating long and short stitches.
- Work a second row of stitches either above or below the first row. As you work across the new row, fill in the gaps left by the short stitches in the previous row, blending the new stitches into the existing stitches.
- Continue working in this way until the required area has been filled in, making sure that all the stitches are worked roughly in the same direction. However, you may need to angle some stitches slightly if you are following an irregular shape. Fasten off the end of the thread on the wrong side.

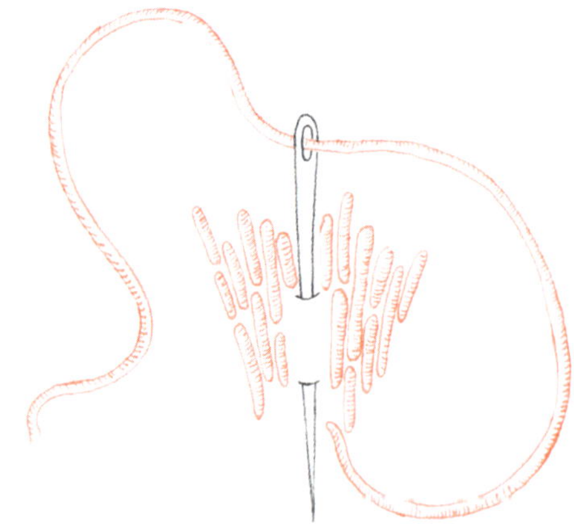

COUCHING

Couching is a really beautiful technique where one or more threads are applied to the surface of the fabric and held in place with small stitches using a complementary or contrasting thread. You can mix thread types, and colours to create endless combinations. We prefer using a thicker thread for the strand laid on the fabric (the couched thread) and a finer thread for the small securing stitches (the couching stitches), and we like using different colours for each thread. Couching is particularly well-suited to sewing outlines as it creates a solid line, but it can also be used for filling in areas by laying the couched threads very close together to make blocks of colour.

HERE'S WHAT YOU DO

- Choose two threads, preferably in different colours or shades. The couched thread should be thicker than the thread you're using for the couching stitches, and at least the length of the desired line/outline plus a little extra for finishing off.
- Thread two embroidery needles with the different threads.
- Make a simple knot in the end of the laid thread, then bring the needle from the wrong side of the fabric through to the right side at the point where you want the embroidery to start. Lay the couched thread along the line or outline to be embroidered.
- Now insert the needle with the thinner couching thread, 3–5mm (⅛–¼in) along from where the laid thread has been brought up to the right side of the fabric. Following the lines of the design, sew the laid thread down using small stitches at approximately 3–5mm (⅛–¼in) intervals. Sew from left to right or vice versa, just make sure you keep the size, direction and spacing of the couching stitches consistent. Keep the laid thread taut so that it doesn't become loose and wavy.
- Once the entire length of the laid thread has been secured to the fabric with couching stitches, pass the needle with the laid thread through to the back, then fasten off the ends of both the couched and couching threads.

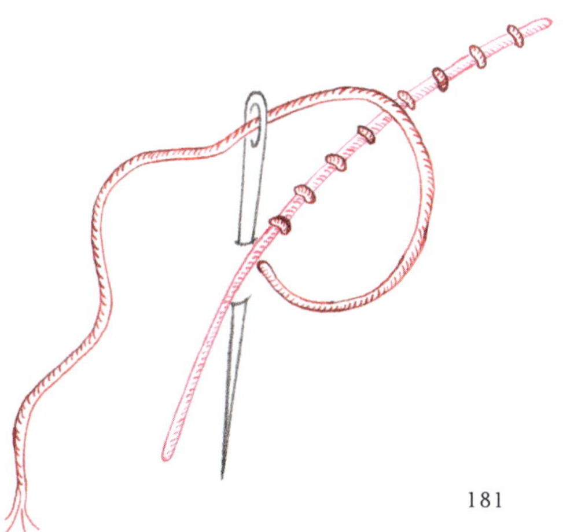

Farewell

Thank you

Thank you for picking up this book. We hope that you now feel inspired to get started with your own embroidery projects, and that perhaps you will view nature through fresh and curious eyes. It has been a huge pleasure for us to make this book; it has helped us get a little closer to nature, and we feel enriched by its beauty and grateful for all the unique designs it has given us.

NATASJA HJERRILD ROSENQUIST

Natasja runs the company and Instagram profile Lille Klode, where she provides inspiration for giving your clothes a longer life through embroidery. Natasja also runs embroidery workshops, where she teaches visible mending and embroidery for beginners.

I am driven by optimizing and refining what already exists. I am fascinated and inspired time and time again by how a piece of discarded clothing can acquire new value with some simple embroidery, new buttons or a nice patch. I love the process of going from an idea to the end result. It feels like a collaboration between the fabric and me – I have to relate to the material and 'listen to the fabric' to understand what is possible. Often, a hole or the location of a mark will speak for itself and determine what design is needed. The feeling of creating something new from something that would otherwise be discarded is almost indescribable – it makes me proud and gives me a sense of deeper meaning, both on a personal and professional level.

If you are curious about my work, follow @lilleklode and visit www.lilleklode.dk, where I share inspiration, offer information about new workshops and sell everything you need to get started with embroidery.

RAGNA MOURITZEN

Ragna Mouritzen is an artist with a Bachelor's degree in Fine Art Drawing from Camberwell College of Arts in London, followed by a Master's in Ceramic Design from the Royal Danish Academy of Fine Arts, Schools of Architecture, Design and Conservation. Since graduating, she has worked both on her own practice and collaborative projects, and has exhibited in Denmark and abroad. She also works in product development for Royal Copenhagen.

In creating this book, I have been enthralled by the possibilities of working with a variety of media. I have been inspired by the different stitches to explore the many ways of creating beautiful, poetic and personal small pieces that you can adorn clothes and other items with. I am interested in craftsmanship, both my own and that of others, and am fascinated by the ways that you can use embroidery to personalize, improve and connect to what you have created.

A SEED WAS SOWN IN 1990

We have actually known each other since we were just three and four years old. We first met when Ragna and her family became Natasja's downstairs neighbours in an almost idyllic housing co-operative in Nørrebro, Copenhagen. We lived next door to each other for ten years, and spent our important childhood years together. Even though we lived in the city, it didn't hold us back from exploring the nature around us, which sparked our creativity. We built caves in willow trees, made perfume out of rose petals and caught insects in jam jars, and every time it rained we found 'diamonds' – that's what we called the raindrops that lay on the leaves in the yard.

As well as playing outside together, we also had a shared thread of creativity. We spent hours tinkering and pottering and drawing and painting. Fortunately, we have both maintained our creative interests. Who would have imagined that now – 35 years later – we would end up writing a book together? Although we have come a long way since then, we agree that the foundations for our creative and artistic lives were laid back then, in that little co-operative in Nørrebro.

With love,
Ragna and Natasja

Published in Denmark as Lille Klode by Forlaget Grønningen 1, 2025.

First published in Great Britain in 2026 by
Ilex, an imprint of
Octopus Publishing Group Ltd
Carmelite House
50 Victoria Embankment
London EC4Y 0DZ
www.octopusbooks.co.uk

An Hachette UK Company
www.hachette.co.uk

The authorized representative in the EEA is Hachette Ireland, 8 Castlecourt Centre, Dublin 15, D15 XTP3, Ireland
(email: info@hbgi.ie)

This edition 2026.

Published in agreement with Forlaget Grønningen 1, Copenhagen.

Distributed in the US by Hachette Book Group, 1290 Avenue of the Americas, 4th and 5th Floors, New York, NY 10104

Distributed in Canada by Canadian Manda Group, 664 Annette St., Toronto, Ontario, Canada M6S 2C8

ISBN: 978-1-84601-705-6
eISBN: 978-1-84601-706-3

A CIP catalogue record for this book is available from the British Library.

Printed and bound in China.

10 9 8 7 6 5 4 3 2 1

Cover and typesetting: Lene Gammelgaard
Photography: Natasja Hjerrild Rosenquist and Ragna Louisa Mouritzen
Illustrations: Ragna Louisa Mouritzen

English edition:
Translator: Ian Giles
Commissioning Editor: Emma Hanson
Editor: Scarlet Furness
Copy Editor: Katie Hardwicke
Art Director: Ben Gardiner
Page Layout: Jeremy Tilston
Production Manager: Caroline Alberti